INFORMATION SIGNALS PROCESSING AND TRANSMITTING

PROF. MICHAEL BANK

PARTRIDGE

To order additional copies of this book, contact
Toll Free +65 3165 7531 (Singapore)
Toll Free +60 3 3099 4412 (Malaysia)
orders.singapore@partridgepublishing.com

www.partridgepublishing.com/singapore

CONTENTS

Conclusion

This book was conceived to explain the problems in the current state of electrical systems and the possible ways to solve them. But it was decided to begin from conclusion. Why is not? After all any writer, and composer or artist knows in beginning of work how will end this work. And many visitors to the theater or concert hall know what they will get. Maybe will be better right away to explain what we will see or hear.

All content can divide on two parts. First - information signal and second - transmitting this signal using electrical systems.

For transmitting large quantity electrical energy today one using tree-phase lines, which have following advantages:

- If they are balanced, they are not radiate signal.
- The source and load of three-phase line are single bloc's ended efficient devices.
- They transmit three one phase signals using three wires.
- But there are and disadvantages also.
- On all length three-phase line one need save 120 degrees phase difference between currents in wires.

- The distances between wires must be the same on all long, therefore are difficult building three- phase line in real conditions.
- These lines are very expensive.
- They are easily damaged, so frequent interruptions in work are possible
- There are many problems when one needs to take part of energy in not three-phase form.
- There are difficult in creating three-phase system on rugged terrain.
- Wires can rich by Calcium. Therefore temperature of wires increases till 100 degrees. Today this is very important due to heating is large problem in the word.
- And there is technical problem of this book. Unfortunately, the correct terminology is not always used in electrical engineering literature. Two examples: first - the names single-phase or two-phase signals do not match the definition of the term phase. And second example. For converter DC to AC, the word inverter is used, although it is known that this process is not inversion.

Foreword

The work presented in this book summarizes a number of new ideas for the transition of electrical and information signals to a new concept. Briefly, this concept can be formulated as follows: "any electrical system, including information, transmitting systems can be built using a single-wire method." After publication methods of real realization these ideas (more than ten years ago), numerous objections, like the following, arose. Any electrical device has at least two input and two output wires. So it is impossible to transmit electricity signals using one wire.

But this is good known that active energy transmitted from source to consumer and does not come back to source. If so, maybe one wire is enough? This idea was proposed by Nicola Tesla. Author with friends checked one-wire system fragments by simulations and measurements of model parameters. Specialists are agreeing that transfer to the one-wire method will give an extremely large profit. But there is a popular objection.

We can get a larger profit in case of three-phase systems reconstruction..

Beginning researchers and students should remember that in our today's world, not everything is invented yet. Besides, if all scientists, professors, engineers, and students are of the same thinking about important problems, it does not mean that their opinion does not need corrections. The success of a new idea or invention does not always depend on money, on the help of big bosses, or on luck. In this book is not proposed the next one perpetual mobile also.

The task of the author is to help the young readers to find and to solve new interesting and useful problems.

Modern method of research in the field of transmission information shows that there is a great reserve in information communication systems efficiency. But before using modern methods we have to know how it is correct to separate the needed information from redundancy[1].

Information Signal

Since the invention of the radio, there has been an exponential increase in transmitted announcements and entertainment programs. The strong wading of frequency channels band pass connected also with transmitting digital signals instead of analogous.

Due to the limiting bandwidth in communication channels, transmitted signals must be compressed. The most difficult problems are found in mobile communication systems, when exists multipath propagation and Doppler Effect, where to prevent these problems, the size of the signal (bit number) is increased. Typical examples of these methods are error correction code, pilot signals, special headers, etc. The common peculiarities of human processing of video and audio information are shown below.

On the other hand, due to the limited bandwidth in communication channels, transmitted signals must be compressed. This begs the question—what should be transmitted in these types of signals, if a large part of them is removed by th compressing system? A human being cannot interpret or remember all signals that are received by the eyes and ears. If the brain were capable of absorbing every bit of information, the brain would reach maximum capacity soon after birth and would not be able to absorb additional information. There are effective compression techniques for removing a large proportion of received redounded signals. This begs the question—why transmits these types of signals if they are removed by the system processor? Since we do not know the manner in which the brain receives impressions, knowledge of algorithm perception enables us to invent new methods for decreasing distortions level. A study of perception algorithm perception will enable the development of new methods for video and sound signal transmission quality. All known methods are based on the measurement of signal variation [12]. Presently, this is not possible due to deliberate signal variation during the compression process. But the most difficult task is to understand the process of perceiving the impression of a work of art.

Video Signal, Physiological Redundancy Examples

Physiological redundancy consists of part of the signal that is not required for perception. It is a proven fact that the system controlling the brain sensor removes a large proportion of information that enters the eyes and ears. However, this type of signal variation is not usually noticeable by an audience.

Let us examine several examples of physiological redundancy found in video and audio signals. A television camera transmits information on each pixel from line to line [2 – 5]. The order in which our eyes view this process is as follows: first we are seeing all contour lines, then the curved loops, and finally the central points. So we are seeing considerable results of "shaking" along contour lines. Subsequently, the eye transmits less quantity of information from positions without clear lines. In other words, a decrease in bit number corresponds to a section of the picture with no clear lines. Another classic example of physiological redundancy is the observation of moving objects. Transmitting 15 pictures only per sec is needed to achieve continuous movement in a moving object. Where the velocity is great, only discrete moments are needed.

Another example of physiological redundancy is color resolution where resolution is smaller than black-white resolution. Through black-white resolution, one can view finer details (three to four pixels). For example, where there are two separate black lines, the distance between the lines must be smaller 1 mm.

Another example of physiological redundancy is color resolution where resolution is smaller than black-white resolution. Through black-white resolution, one can view finer details (three to four pixels).

Vision Perception System Models

In the case of video signals, compression is more effective when searching for objects that require more detailed transmission (including contours, lines, central points, and periodic forms). Communication between the brain and the eye's pupil enables the brain to remove statistical redundancy and to gain control upon the movement of the pupil for achieving image perception through a minimum number of bits (see Figure 7). The eye can receive a great amount of information (more than 1 Gbit/s). However, only a small part of this information is received by the brain (approximately 100 bit/s)

Why only 100bit/s? Numerous psychological experiments indicate that during a period of 0.7 seconds, the brain calculates the details of an image at the rate of 70 bits/s. We can perceive different parts in a painting within a given time frame of less than 0.8 s. The brain calculates this at the rate of 80 bits/s. Maximal reading speed is 30–40 bit/s. The conclusion here is that the brain receives impressions at the rate of less than 100 bits/s.

Audio Signal psychological redundancy examples

Sounds cannot be heard during 100 ms after volume peak and 5 ms before volume peak. One cannot hear small spectral components, whereas maximal components can be heard because of a significantly greater difference in frequency (see Figure 9 in [11]). This is termed "masking effect," which is used in most audio signal compression methods [8–10].

The masking effect has been researched extensively. Critical frequency band tables divide bandwidths into critical frequency bands where the masking effect is used (see Figure 10 in [11]). Following spectral transformation of real sound signals, we can transmit only one or two maximal components of each critical frequency band.

Figure 10 masking effect experimental data. This case correspond to one spectral component (1000 Hz) [11] 2.3 Model of Human Hearing Perception

Let us assume audio signal consists of short stationary fragments, as illustrated in Figure 11. These fragments vary after time t1, t2, etc. If we take other fragments according to constant times t1, t2. . . as in all of today's audio compression systems, we will obtain complicated spectrums. In this case, transfer takes place from one stationary signal to the other. If we take stationary fragments (times t1, t2 . . .), we will obtain simple spectrums. Subsequently, the information quantity

4

of signal in spectral form depends on choosing the method of time interval. Maybe this feedback from brain to hearing processor is explanation of strong rhythm influence.

Figure 11 in [11] - time intervals choosing. The following are three important points worth considering:

- The ear membrane consists of 23,000 resonators and operates similar to a spectral analyzer.
- The brain receives a small amount of spectral components.
- There can be no music or even speech without rhythm. In addition, rhythm is a quality that we physically sense and is not only something we hear. We propose a hearing system model (see Figure 12 in [11]) that operates within frequency and time domains simultaneously. The system divides signals into fragments corresponding to stationary signals.

The system conducts spectral transformation and finally leaves only the maximal components in each critical frequency bands.

Figure 12 in [11] is hearing system model: (1) resonators, (2) encoders, (3) channel between ear and brain, (4) central processing unit, (5) spacing feedback.

The more information in arts music, painting, or architecture, corresponds to human vision and to system models of hearing perception, the more enhanced will be the impression. The brain's volume (cell) is limited in receiving information (see Figure 13 in [11]). The receptor-brain system partially removes redundancy. The task of this system is to compress received signals even if the data is of a greater size than the cell volume of the brain. This dissonance gives us a sense of uneasiness. For greater reception of impressions and agreeable perceptions, we must achieve maximal statistical redundancy of input signals. For this purpose, the fine arts implement predictable lines, elementary forms, recurrent (rhythmic) figures, predictable colors, and repetition of some of the fragments. Music implements clear rhythm and emphasizes frequencies that correspond to the critical frequency band center.

Our memory system operates according to patterns or samples, as follows: closed loop with emphases center, separate form, construction part, melody, and rhythmical picture. If we want to store image information, then fewer bits are required as opposed to memorizing separate bits. In information theory, this compression method is termed "alphabet extension" or "using a codebook." People usually wait for patterns to be perfected through repetition since this helps in better remembering images. A small variation in repetition—slight difference in the eyes, nonsymmetrical face, nonsymmetrical build, slight variation in rhythm, or volume repeated melodies or phrases—can produce the strongest impressions. We can find confirmation in famous works of art. Artists, sculptors, architects, and composers have emphasized, by intuitive perception, the peculiarities above. Numerous examples are listed below. Increasing redundancy in visual and audio signals.

Now we come to paradoxical conclusion. If one need increase impression one need increase redundancy. To decrease the number of bits for transmitting the visual signal and simultaneously for increasing statistical redundancy, it is necessary to implement predictable lines and figures (that have large autocorrelation). It is a known fact that the ratio of size dimensions corresponds to Fibonacci numbers or to additional serial or to golden section are more attractive. Here the following elements arithmetically depend from previous elements. Throughout history, the ratio for length to width of rectangles of 1.61803 39887 49894 84820 has been considered the most pleasing to the eye. This ratio was named the golden ratio by the Greeks. In the world of mathematics, the numeric value is called "phi," named for the Greek sculptor Phidias.

The space between the columns forms golden rectangles. There are golden rectangles throughout this structure that is found in Athens, Greece.

It is known that the ratio taken for half of the perimeter size and the pyramid height equals π. Use of the gold section increases redundancy due to the high predictability of neighboring lines or forms.

The greatest artists "know" this theory. For example on many portraits the part of portrait around a face consists of repeated fragments with large redundancy. Conjugate (coupled, additional) colors are another source of redundancy implementation of conjugate colors. The sum of two conjugate colors gives color near to white.

The same methods are used in music also.

The strings sound includes overtones. Overtone is sound with double frequency, for example, f 2f 4f 8f . .

Sounds (notes) are divided by octaves. Each melody can be performed in selected octave. Inside of each octave, we have m = 12 tones. Out of 12 tones, 8 tones are used that correspond to tonality. All this simultaneously sounding 8 quota; increasing redundancy. The "masking effect" must decrease the smaller component in one critical band. If you hearing two sound in critical band so you hearing dissonance. The critical frequency band is approximately 16% of central frequency. The proof of this explanation is illustrated below in table.

The musical composition consists of melodies. Melody has a large autocorrelation. This allows us to predict subsequent tones in the melody. Thus, a melody signal has large redundancy. We remember a melody by repetition of the same melody. In other words, the melody is played not only once, but many times over. Both the composer and the performer slightly change the melody during repetition, without a variation in "content." The following parameters can be changed: volume, use of instruments, micro pauses, etc. These variations increase redundancy and help to create a greater impression. There are many musical examples of prominent composers who have made successful use of melody repetition, for example, Ravel's "Bolero" or the first section of Shostakovich's Seventh Symphony (Leningrad). Rhythm holds great importance in the construction of a musical composition. There can be no music without rhythm. Rhythm helps us to perceive audio signals like in stationary fragment sequences with large redundancy. The poetry, which is defined to a large extent byrhythm, has greater influence on people than simple text. As a matter of fact, people look for rhythms in all kinds of sounds, for example, in the swishing sound of a car's windscreen wipers or in communal prayer or when listening to the tweets of birds. Here we can make a rough estimation of human perception audio signal compression rate. We can hear K = 23,000 different frequencies. Maximal entropy equals log223000 ≈ 14.5. The note quantity is 240. In one tonality, it will be 12. Notes in the middle octave have maximum probability. Notes that correspond to basic tone (tonic) have the highest probability. The entropy of note distribution is approximately 0.1. If we take into consideration the differential method for transmitting seriate melodies, we will get H (A) ≈ 0.02 or χ ≈ 99.8%. So the compression rate is ≈ 500. It is interesting to note that there is another item that is common to painting and music. To achieve good acoustic conditions, a room is required with a golden section between length (L), width (B), and height (H) (see Figure 15 in [11].

In Jerusalem there is a sculpture of the golden section. The length of all lines corresponds to the Fibonacci numbers.

Fig 1 Golden section in Jerusalem

How to Give an Effective Speech

According to Wikipedia, oratory is the art of public speaking. In ancient Greece and Rome, oratory was studied as a component of rhetoric (that is, composition and delivery of speeches) and was an important skill in public and private life. Aristotle and Quintilian discussed oratory; and the subject, with definitive rules and models, was emphasized as a part of a "complete education" during the Middle Ages and Renaissance.

Below are special rules for putting together a speech, which are original and unexpected in their nature.

- After attending a lecture, the average person will remember about 10% of what was talked about. Therefore, it is of paramount importance that this 10% includes the main idea you wish to get across to your audience.
- Do not begin your speech blatantly disproving present theories, which are generally accepted.

Rather, mention that present theories hold valuable information, and then mention your innovative method.

- In the first quarter of the lecture, prove your ideas by expounding them. Next, give examples, analogies, and mention other people's opinions in order to bring increased clarity to these new ideas.
- Try to be as convincing as possible when giving a lecture, even to the point where the listener asks himself, "Yes, this makes sense. Why didn't I see this before?"
- When a listener finds it easy to absorb and understand what is being said, he is more likely to go along and to agree to what you are saying and putting forward in your speech.
- Good organization is vital, and it is best to plan and write up what you intend to say in your speech. Nevertheless, do not read out the speech word for word. Rather, if you have carried

out your planning correctly, the words in your speech should flow smoothly.

- Try not to include superfluous words. Do not make repetition of words and phrases, such as "well," "basically," "the truth of the matter is," etc.
- It is possible to increase volume a little. If you find that your argument is rather weak.
- Look at the faces of the members of the audience. Do not let your eyes wander or gaze on the walls or on what's occurring outside the window.
- Conclude your lecture by repeating the main ideas.
- The new information presented in your speech should represent 10% of what you say. The rest is redundancy. Therefore, it is worth your while to stress and to further expound upon the main 10% of your speech.
- Try to think of something influential to say for your closing sentence. The audience pays particular attention to the final words that are uttered by the orator.

The above points are not new. In fact, they were recommended long ago. They are a testament to the following common rule: "For success in public speaking, one must use redundancy correctly."

Autism Problems

Autism is a brain development disorder that impairs social interaction and communication and causes restricted and repetitive behavior, all starting before a child is three years old. This set of signs distinguishes autism from milder autism spectrum disorders (ASD) such as Asperser's syndrome. In the second and third years, autistic children have less frequent and less diverse babbling, consonants, words, and word combinations; their gestures are less often integrated with words. Autistic children are less likely to make requests or share experiences and are more likely to simply repeat others' words or reverse pronouns. Joint attention seems to be necessary for functional speech, and deficits in joint attention seem to distinguish infants with ASD. For example, they may look at a [11] pointing hand instead of the pointed-at object, and they consistently fail to point to "comment" about or "share" an experience at age-appropriate times. Autistic children may have difficulty with imaginative play and with developing symbols into language. It may be that children diagnosed with autism have difficulties deleting redundancy. Habitual speech for them sounds dissonant. They have difficulties verbalizing their thoughts, and often their speech is very simple and lacking depth [11] and [3]. Perhaps we must communicate with these people using minimum redundancy. Instead of detailed and image-

Be airing descriptions, one can use simple telegraphed text or poem-style text. This is especially important in the teaching process.

The information, experimental results, assumptions, and hypotheses within this piece of writing bring us to a paradoxical conclusion: to increase the influence of a newly created work of art and receive maximal impressions, we must decrease information quantity in signals between signals from the art object and up to observer or listener. The greater part of the signal is intended for redundancy.

- We must implement lines, figures, word patterns, and combinations of notes with large autocorrelation.

Rhythm, which is an essential component in music and speech, is also a desirable quality in paintings.

- Rhythm uses separate patterns, clear contours, melodies, etc.
- It is possible to increase impressions with the help of pattern sound repetition, especially where the differences between each repetition are in a subtle manner.
- Rhythm, which is an essential component in music and speech, is also a desirable quality in paintings;
- Rhythm uses separate patterns, clear contours, and melodies etc, which include finer bits of information.

There is an additional conclusion which may not be considered scientific.

It is conceivable that millions of years ago, as a result of mutation, a distinctive class of monkey entered the universe that was able to analyze received information in a more subtle manner.

This monkey was not only Table to receive danger signal so to experience various motions,

Including "love", but also had the ability for deleting redundancy by its brain system. This cu lminated in receiving information in a manner which made more efficient use of stored information, and in the enhanced ability of comparison between new and stored information.

Perhaps this mutation contributed to a great extent in the transformation of the monkey in to a human being. Maybe changes between information and redundancy are additional possibility increasing impression from art. And further. Redundancy is not something superfluous. It is a necessary part of perception that determines the impression of a work of art or of nature. The author agrees with those who believe that art is not what is fashionable today, but what remains.

Conclusion to parts 3 - 5

The information, experimental results, assumptions, and hypotheses within this piece of writing bring us to a paradoxical conclusion:

To increase the influence of a newly released work of art and receive maximal impressions, we must increase ratio redundancy / information quantity in signals.

To this end:

- We must implement lines, figures, word patterns, and combinations of notes with large autocorrelation;

- Rhythm, which is an essential component in music and speech, is also a desirable quality in paintings;
- Rhythm uses separate patterns, clear contours, and melodies etc, which include finer bits of information.
- It is possible to increase impressions with the help of pattern/ sound repetition, especially where the differences between each repetition are minimal.

There is an additional conclusion which may not be considered scientific.

It is conceivable that millions of years ago, as a result of mutation, a distinctive class of monkey entered the universe that was able to analyze received information in a more subtle manner. This monkey was not only able to receive danger signals or to experience various emotions, including "love", but also had the ability for deleting redundancy by its brain system. This culminated in receiving information in a manner which made more efficient use of stored information, and in the enhanced ability of comparison between new and stored information.

Perhaps this mutation contributed to a great extent in the transformation of the monkey into a human being.

Maybe ratio between information and redundancy are additional possibility increasing Impression from art.

Single-Wire Electric Transmission Line In Patents

Today is changing not only what we transmitting, but how we it transmitting. As was written before, in part 2, the more perspective method is one wire method.

Here we will show principles and implementations this method by patents texts. Maybe this describing will help to beginning engineers.

But there is one problem here. The drawings in the patents are very small. However, they are repeated in the book [18]

Let us begin from main patent in our problems.

- *SINGLE-WIRE ELECTRIC TRANSMISSION LINE*

Publication number: 20140152123

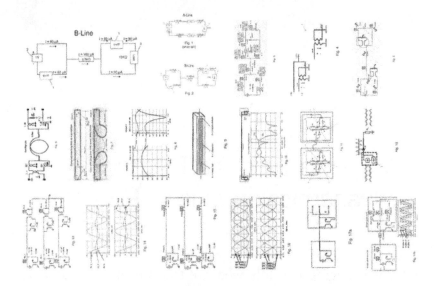

Figures A

CROSS-REFERENCE TO RELATED APPLICATIONS

This application is a Continuation-in-Part of International Application No. PCT/IL2012/000291 filed Aug. 2, 2012, designating the United States and claiming priority to U.S. Provisional Application No. 61/514,906, filed Aug. 4, 2011, the disclosures of both foregoing applications being incorporated herein by reference in their entireties.

FIELD OF THE INVENTION

The present invention relates to the field of electrical system. More particularly, the invention relates to an electrical transmission system which uses only a single-wire electric transmission line while eliminating the need to use the ground or another wire as commonly used as a second line.

BACKGROUND OF THE INVENTION

Usually in books, articles, or lectures authors explain the work of an electrical circuit (A-Line) as the process of current flowing from the generator to the load by one wire, and then back to the generator by another wire. But it is known that free-access electrons move relatively slowly, and the electrical energy is transmitted at light speed. Actually today's wires electric system uses two or more channels (wires) for transmitting energy or information. While in both channels there is the same information. It is known that active (real) power does not return from load to the generator. From this point of view may be does not need second channel in electrical system. In other words may be a line of electric system can be a single wire.

In the prior-art, there were attempts to perform electrical energy transmission by means of one wire. First applications of the single-wire electrical energy transmission were disclosed by Nikola Tesla in U.S. Pat. No. 1,119,736 and in British Patent No. 8,200. Another single line transmission technique is known as the Goubau line or G-line for short, which is a type of single-wire transmission line which is used at UHF and microwave frequencies (see Geog Goubau, "Surface waves and their Application to Transmission Lines," Journal of Applied Physics, Volume 21, November, 1950). However, a G-line is a type of waveguide, rather than a wire in an electric circuit. There was experiment based on the Russian patent application 1993 year by Stanislaw and Konstantin Avramenko. All these proposals are based on signal processing like frequency up converting or signal straightening. These processing influences on transmitting information and lead to power lose.

19

There is also an electricity distribution method using only one conductor, but with the participation of earth. This method is known as the Single Wire Earth Return (SWER). However, the simplification of the energy transfer in this system is achieved due to the loss of part the power produced by the source.

It is well known advantages of three-phase system where energy transmitted by four wires. The presence of four wires is not the only drawback of three-phase system. Another drawback may be the fact that line voltage between two wires in this system at the root of the three above of phase voltage. This may have negative consequences, given such a corona effect and additional losses in the lines.

It is an object of the present invention to provide an electric system which is capable of using a single-wire channel for transmitting energy or information without signal form changing and additional loses.

It is another object of the present invention to provide an electrical system that does not use the ground instead of the second wire.

Other objects and advantages of the invention will become apparent as the description proceeds.

SUMMARY OF THE INVENTION

The present invention relates to a single-wire electric transmission line system, which comprises:

The present invention further relates to a single-wire electric transmission line system, which comprises two phase-shifting devices, coupled to each of the poles of the power source in such a manner that each of said phase-shifting device shifts the phase of a first signal propagating through said pole and the phase of a second signal propagating through the other pole such that the shifted phases of both signals will be essentially identical, and such that the shifted signals are added with essentially the same phase, whenever both poles are connected together to form a single-wire, through which the resulting added signal propagates.

According to an embodiment of the invention, the phase-shifting device(s) is an inverter that shifts the phase of its corresponding pole by +90 degrees, −90 degrees or by 180 degrees, such that the shifted signal(s) is added with essentially the same phase.

According to an embodiment of the invention, the phase-shifting device is a transformer with opposite windings.

According to an embodiment of the invention, one of the two phase-shifting devices is a Low Pass Filter (LPF) and the other phase-shifting device is a High Pass Filter (HPF).

According to an embodiment of the invention, the phase-shifting device is an essentially half period delay line with respect to the length of the line that is connected to the other pole of the source. For example, the delay line is one-port strip line including metal wire on dielectric, which lying on a metallic padding.

According to an embodiment of the invention, the phase-shifting device(s) is a digital module adapted for performing phase shifting. For example, the digital module is a Hilbert transform device.

According to an embodiment of the invention, in the case of a DC signal, the phase-shifting device runs as two capacitors connected in turn to charge through the keys to one of the outputs of a bipolar DC power supply, a second end connected to the power of the capacitor is grounded, the end of the capacitor disconnected from the source, who at the time of charging was grounded is connected to another output bipolar DC power supply and to the input of a single-line, the other end of the capacitor is grounded.

According to an embodiment of the invention, the single-wire is connected to a corresponding single-wire load module that includes a two polar load and phase-shifting device coupled to one polar of said load, by splitting said single-wire into two lines, such that one line is coupled to said phase-shifting device and the other line is coupled to the load, in such a manner that currents are flow in both lines, but in opposite phases with respect to one another.

According to an embodiment of the invention, the single-wire is split into three wires, wherein each of said three wires is connected to a different pole of a three-phase load via a corresponding phase-shifting device, in order to form a single-wire three-phase system, in the following manner:

According to an embodiment of the invention, the first phase-shifting device of the three-phase system is an inductance resistance and the second phase-shifting device of said three-phase system is a capacitor resistance.

In another aspect the invention relates to a single-wire load (instead of ordinary two wires load), which comprises:

BRIEF DESCRIPTION OF THE DRAWINGS

In the drawings A:

FIG. 1.A schematically illustrates an example of conventional electric system (A-line), according to the prior-art;

FIG. 2.A schematically illustrates a single-wire electric system (B-Line) that is equivalent to the A-line system of FIG. 1.A, according to an embodiment of the present invention;

FIG. 3.A is a print out of the simulation results of the B-Line system of FIG. 2.A;

FIG. 4.A schematically illustrates a phase-shifting device in form of a transformer, according to an embodiment of the present invention;

FIG. 5.A is a print out of the simulation result of a B-Line system with the transformer of FIG. 4.A;

FIG. 6.A schematically illustrates a scheme of B-Line model with dividing transformers;

FIG.7.A schematically illustrates a conventional high frequency long line and its B-Line equivalent implementation;

FIG. 8.A the simulation results of the long line and its B-Line equivalent of FIG. 7.A;

FIG. 9.A schematically illustrates an exemplary one-port strip line for frequency of 2.3 GHz;

FIG. 10.A is a graph showing the B-Line with the one-port strip line for frequency 2.3 GHz of FIG. 9.A and its simulations results;

FIG. 11.A schematically illustrates an exemplary implementation of a DC B-Line circuit, according to an embodiment of the present invention;

FIG. 12.A schematically illustrates using one-pole source principle, according to an embodiment of the present invention;

FIG. 13.A schematically illustrates an exemplary implementation of a B-Line three-phase scheme, according to an embodiment of the present invention;

FIG. 14.A is a graph showing the simulation results of the B-Line three-phase scheme of FIG. 13.A;

FIG. 15.A schematically illustrates an exemplary implementation of B-Line three-phase scheme with one pole generators, according to an embodiment of the present invention;

FIG. 16.A is a graph showing the simulation results of the B-Line three-phase scheme of FIG. 5.A, 15.A; and 5.17a.A and 5.17b.A schematically illustrate an exemplary implementation of B-Line three-phase scheme with one pole generators and typical three-phase load.

All figures more detailed described in [18]

DETAILED DESCRIPTION OF THE INVENTION

Throughout this description the term "B-Line" is used to indicate an electrical circuit as the process of current flowing from the generator to the load by one wire. This term does not imply any particular arrangement or components, and invention is applicable to all suitable configurations of electrical circuits.

First concept—today one can read another explanation as the process of current flowing. Not like from the generator to the load, and then back to the generator. But this explanation is following: "Two potentials derive from two terminal of source with opposite phases to two terminals of load with light speed." So energy flows in one direction.

Second concept—using ground instead of one wire can be for very short distance only; because the earth resistance is much larger than the resistance of copper. According to the resistance of the earth can be from 5 to 5000 ohms per meter. In many electrical systems grounding is used to potential zeroing. An electrical ground system should have an appropriate current-carrying capability to serve as an adequate zero-voltage reference level. In electronic circuit theory, a "ground" is usually idealized as an infinite source or sinks for charge, which can absorb an unlimited amount of current without changing its potential. The current flows into the ground and spreads out in an endless ground, as is the case with a protective earth. In the case of protective grounding, if an accident happens, the current anywhere in the other place does not get. The main characteristic of the grounding resistance is spreading current, i.e., a resistance that the earth (ground) has a current spreading at the site of this current. Land spreading is a ground area that surrounds the grounding electrodes, in which the boundary of the current density is so low that potential, which has virtually no land, depends on the current flowing from the electrodes. That is why outside of this boundary current can always be equated to zero. In other words, if one point of scheme connected to ground, it does not mean that the energy or the information is transmitted to another point scheme, which is also connected to ground. Both points have potential equal zero.

Third concept—If one would like to get adequate electrical energy transmitting system processing, one need to do that source and load can "see" the same resistances. And load current mast is the same that is match to Ohm low.

Reference will now be made to several embodiments of the present invention(s), examples of which are illustrated in the accompanying figures. Wherever practicable similar or like reference numbers may be used in the figures and may indicate similar or like functionality. The figures depict embodiments of the present invention for purposes of illustration only. One skilled in the art will readily recognize from the following description that alternative embodiments of the structures and methods illustrated herein may be employed without departing from the principles of the invention described herein.

The terms, "for example," "e.g.," "optionally," as used herein, are intended to be used to introduce non-limiting examples. While certain references are made to certain example system components or services, other components and services can be used as well and/or the example components can be combined into fewer components and/or divided into further components.

It will be better to explain the main idea of a single-wire electric system of the present invention (i.e., B-Line) by comparison with a conventional electric system (i.e., A-Line). FIGS. 1 and 2 schematically illustrate an A-Line circuit and a B-Line circuit, respectively. Both circuits include a common power source 2 (e.g., 1 volt generator), a load 3 (e.g., R=10 kOhm) and the currents is about 90 microamperes (I≈90 μA). At the A-Line circuit the lines resistance is about 1 kOhm, and at the B-Line circuit, the resistance of the single-wire transmission line is about 0.5 kOhm as will be described in further details hereinafter. The equivalent B-Line circuit includes a first phase shifter **1** coupled to one poles of the power source **2** and a second phase shifter coupled to one of the poles of the load **3**.

The B-Line system of the present invention is based on the assumption that it would be possible to combine two wires (i.e., the electric lines running out from the first pole and the second pole of a power source) if currents would be of the same amplitudes and same phases. For example, this can be achieved by inserting a phase-shifting device (i.e., the phase shifter **1**) in one of the lines. The phase-shifting device shifts the phase of a first signal propagating through that line such that the shifted phase of the first signal will be essentially identical to the phase of a second signal propagating through the other line. For instance, 10 milliseconds delay line can be used for signal with a frequency of 50 Hz. After the phase-shifting device, phases and amplitudes of the currents in both lines are essentially identical. Thus, at the generator side (i.e., at the power source **2** side), both lines can be combined into a single wire, such that the shifted first signal is added to the second signal with essentially the same phase of the second signal, whenever both lines are connected together to form a single-wire, through which the resulting added signal propagates (i.e., the sum of the currents from both lines).

At the load side, the single wire splits into two wires (i.e., two lines), and similarly to the generator side, a phase-shifting device (i.e., a second phase shifter **1**) can be inserted before the load **3** in one of the split wires in order to ensure a normal functionality of the load **3**. As a result, the two conventional wire system (FIG. 1.A) turns into one-way B-Line system (FIG. 2.A), but the power source **2.A** and the load **3** will "see" the conventional two wires system (i.e., A-Line).

According to an embodiment of the invention, the needed phase shift can be achieved by means of a phase-shifting device in form of a delay line, a transformer with opposite windings, low pass and high pass filters, digital phase shifters such as Hilbert transform device(s), etc. For example, if a delay line is used as a phase-shifting device, then its delay must correspond to half period. In the case of 50 or 60 Hz frequencies it is practically impossible using delay line, recall that wire, which corresponds to half wave length, has length equals 3000 or 2500 km. It is convenient on low frequencies to use transformer with opposite windings as phase shifter. As for high frequencies the good solution is delay line.

The main idea of the single-wire electric transmission line of the present invention was supported on ADS and CST simulations programs. Series of simulations with different phase shifters and various resistance lines were carried out. Each simulation was carried out for the A-Line and the B-Line. For clarity, FIGS. 1–3 show the conditions and the simulation results including polarity and magnitude of currents.

That's one of the simulations for the verification of Ohm's law in the proposed scheme (see FIG 5.1). In this typical A-Line circuit, current amplitude everywhere should be 90 μA, wherein 0.5 kOhm is the lines resistance.

In the proposed B-Line scheme (see FIG. 2), we added phase two shifting devices the first at the input and the second at the output, and combined the two lines. As a result a line resistance is 0.5 kOhm.

The simulation shows that the currents at the input and output have not changed. The polarity of the load current depends on where the phase-shifting devices are at the top or bottom.

One can see on FIG. 3 the simulation results of the B-Line system of FIG. 2. For example, in case the phase-shifting device is a transformer with opposite windings, then reverse one wire current phase by the transformer can be reset the current flowing from the winding only. Simply connect the windings cannot be, otherwise the current from one winding to another will flow and the transformer will not perform its functions. As in other similar cases, zeroing can be done with earth (see "Circuit Grounds and Grounding Practices," George Hunka, Undergraduate Laboratory, Dept. of EE, University of Pennsylvania). As will be shown in the following section, the land is not involved in the transfer of energy from the source to the load.

FIG. 4 schematically illustrates a phase-shifting device that can be used in conjunction with the invention. In this embodiment, the phase-shifting device is in form of a transformer. The phase-shifting device illustrated in this figure is particularly convenient because it can be easily applied to low frequency systems. The phase-shifting device is generally indicated by numeral 1 in the figures.

FIG. 5 is print out that shows the results of a B-Line circuit simulation with two units of inverter 1 (as indicated by the transformers TF1 and TF2). The first transformer TF2 is coupled to an AC voltage source SRC 1 (as indicated by numeral 2) and the second transformer TF1 is coupled to the load 3 (as indicated by the resistor RI). One can see on FIG. 5 B-Line circuit with ideal 1:1 transformers simulation.

If the B-Line is used in a system with raising or lowering the voltage, the inverter **1** must be used in both lines. In the one line is used as the transformer with the same included windings (as indicated by transformer TF**2**) and in the second line with opposite included windings (as indicated by transformer TF**1**). The grounding in FIG. 5.5 is zeroing and therefore it is not used and cannot be used as the return path (i.e., the second line). There are several evidences that the earth is not involved in the transfer of power, although one of any evidence would be enough. The main evidence is that the current in B-Line equals to double current in normal scheme and corresponds to Ohm low. So it is impossible any additional current.

Obviously, in the case of a normal two-wire circuit where the source gives 1 V and a load resistance is 50 ohms the current will be equal to 20 mA. For example, in the case of the B-Line circuit like in FIG. 5.5 the current in wire should be 40 mA.

With the aim of experimental verification of the proposed solutions were prepared a number of models. Details of the layout mounted on a wooden board, as a zeroing-grounding used electrical network protective grounding. All voltages and currents in the model coincided with the results of the simulation. To eliminate possible doubts about the possible involvement of the land in signal transduction through the neutral wire three-phase system was tested model with dividing (isolating) transformer at the input. This model scheme is shown in FIG. 6. The model shown in FIG. 6 continued to operate normally and when it was taken out of the receiving part of the laboratory at a distance of about 80 meter and used as a grounding metal rod.

B-Line on High Frequency

Let us show that B-line idea is correct for the high frequency too. On frequency 50 Hz simulations where made by ADS program. This program allows simulating different elements but not electrical lines. So for electrical lines simulations was used element like delay line. On height frequencies one can implement CST program. This program allows simulating different elements including electrical lines.

First we compare normal long line with characteristic impedance 300 Ohm with B-Line on frequency 1.1 GHz. Both models are shown in FIG. 5.7, wherein FIG. 8 shows the simulation results of models **1** and **2** of FIG. 7, on frequency of 1 GHz (as indicated by parameters S11 and S21). On 1.1 GHz it was possible to make delay lines by lines with long equals half wave long. Parameter S21 is the same practically. Parameter S11 of model **2** is better than S11 of model **1**. One can see on FIG. 8 on 1.1 GHz S11 of B-Line is −20 dB and of normal long line is −10 dB. This means that in case of B-line all energy goes from source to load (i.e., there is no power loss).

In high frequency it is possible to make delay line like one-port strip line, e.g., as shown with respect to FIG. 9. With this strip line was made simulation of one wire long line. The simulation results in terms of S-parameter (S1 and S2) magnitude (in dB) are shown in the graph of FIG. 10. The matching long the line is infinitely wide band passes (see appendix about eternal resonance system). This is an advantage, but also disadvantages. There is an advantage because you can pass on a long line of multiple signals with different frequencies. However, in a real system there is always some noise. Even if noise is weak, but in an infinitely wide band it will be infinitely large noise (of course, if the noise is white). Of course, you can apply a filter at the input of the receiver. But this is often problematic. The filter introduces loss and increases the noise factor.

The proposed single-wire system (B-Line) is a selective system. The disadvantage of B-Line is a need to change the delay line in case of change of frequency. B-Line is compatible with the source and load, and in this sense no different from the usual long line. It is selective, but rather broadband. It has no requirements of symmetry, which is often a problem in the prior-art systems when using long line inside the apparatus, where can be different influences on each wire. and DC B-Line

To implement the inverter **1** in a DC circuitry it requires a different solution then the aforementioned transformers. According to an embodiment of the invention, it is proposed to use two capacitors and corresponding switches to implement the inverter **1** (as shown with respect to FIG. 11 in the source side **2** and correspondingly at the load side **3**). Each of the inverter **1** operates as follows: In one period the first capacitor is charges and the second is discharged. In second period they switch functions. Charging current is in one direction, but discharging current direction is reversed.

In this embodiment, in line current has one direction, positive or negative. In this figure, the direction is positive. The resistance value is usually set. So first and second period's duration can only be choosing by value of the capacitors. For example, such a DC B-Line system can be implemented in an electrical railway system (i.e., tramway). In this case, it is possible to transmit electrical power only in wire or only in the rails.

One-Pole Source

The idea of B-Line system allows defining another new element of an electrical circuit—one-pole generator (i.e., source). If we will allocate the connection of the generator and the converter in B-Line scheme, we can talk about unipolar source (as indicated by dotted line in FIG. 5. 12) where one load terminal is connected to a single-wire and the second load terminal is grounded (connected to zero voltage). In this case there is no loss of energy, as all the current coming from a single line passes through the load.

B-Line (One wire) Three-Phase Systems

According to some embodiment of the invention, the suggested B-Line concept allows building unbalanced three-phase system where currents in all phases do not depend on loads in another phases. FIG. 5.13 schematically illustrates a B-Line three-phase scheme with loads 10, 50 and 200 Ohm. Moreover, this B-Line three-phase scheme uses three wires only. The simulation results of this B-Line three-phase scheme are shown in FIG. 5.15). The simulation results on FIG. 14 show that each current depends only on its load, but not like in common three-phase system.

According to another embodiment of the invention, the B-Line three-phase system can be built without using of inverters in the receiving parts (as shown with respect to FIG. 15 and to its corresponding simulation results as shown in FIG. 16). Actually this scheme uses one pole generators. As one can see in the graph of FIG. 16, the current values are by two times smaller than currents value in scheme with reflectors in receiving parts. But generators currents are smaller by two times too. Therefore there is no power loses in this scheme too. It is possible to combine one-pole source through one wire with normal three-phase load by implementing 1200 phase shifters, as seen in FIGS. 5. 17a– 5.17 b.

According to another embodiment, the single-wire may be split into three wires, where each of the three wires is connected to a different pole of a three-phase load via a corresponding phase-shifting device, in order to form a single-wire three-phase system. Accordingly, a first phase-shifting device is coupled to one of the poles of the three-phase load in such a manner that the first phase-shifting device shifts the phase of a first signal propagating through the pole by +60° (e.g., by using a filter). A second phase-shifting device is coupled to the second pole of the three-phase toad in such a manner that the second phase-shifting device shifts the phase of a second signal propagating through the second pole by −60° (e.g., by using a filter). A third phase-shifting device is coupled to the third pole of the three-phase load in such a manner that the third phase-shifting device shifts the phase of a third signal propagating through the third pole by 180° (e.g., by using an inverter). This way, a phase shift of 120° between signals is obtained with minimal energy loss (compared to shifting the phase of the signals by 120° using filters), since the filters are used to shift the phase of the signals only by ±60°.

It should be indicated that if it is desired to protect power lines (cables) there is an option to use a technique where conventional 3 phase high-voltage power lines which extend along a pipe and buried in the ground. However, the high voltage between phases requires substantially separating between them and therefore, the only solution is using 3 insulating pipes (each cable in a separate pipe), to allow sufficient distance between pipes, such that the electric and magnetic field of each line will not induce disturbing currents in the neighboring lines. However, this solution is costly, due to the fact that it is impossible to put all 3 cables in a single pipe. The single-wire electric transmission line system, proposed by the present invention allows using a single high voltage cable (carrying 3 phases) which is extended along a single insulating pipe and buried in the ground, since there are no neighboring lines. This way, the power line is protected against falling trees, rain and falling snow, with relatively low cost, comparing to the need to bury 3 lines.

As will be appreciated by the skilled person the arrangement described in the figures results in an electrical circuit which uses only a single-wire electric transmission line. One-Way system for connection between source and load by one line—(i.e., B-Line) was proposed and checked by simulations and experiments. One way system can be easily implemented as One-pole source, DC B-Line, LF B-Line, HF B-Line, B-Line three-phase system, etc.

It is possible to suppose that using one-way method (i.e., B-Line) can considerable decrease the electrical lines cost. Moreover, B-Line method allows decreasing energy loss in high-voltage electric transmission lines. An additional advantage provided by the invention is that it is possible to achieve decreasing of electrical lines radiation, including Corona effect, so far as one of radiation courses in two lines and three-phase systems have high voltage between lines. Furthermore, B-Line method allows simplifying the high-frequency long lines and improving their options, including easing the requirements for symmetry, good matching and selective properties. Finally, B-Line method also allows building antennas with one radiated element (monopole) equivalent to two element antenna (dipole).

All the above description and examples have been given for the purpose of illustration and are not intended to limit the invention in any way. Many different mechanisms, methods of analysis, electronic and logical elements can be employed, all without exceeding the scope of the invention.

Claims [7]

1. A single-wire electric transmission line system that is composed of the following:

    a. a power source having first and second poles

    b. a phase-shifting device, coupled to one of the poles of said power source so that said phase-shifting device shifts the phase of a first signal propagating through said pole and the shifted phase of said first signal will be essentially identical to the phase of a second signal propagating through the other pole, and such that the shifted first signal is added to the second signal with essentially the same phase of second signal, whenever both poles are connected together to form a single wire through which the resulting added signal propagates

    c. two phase-shifting devices, coupled to each of the poles of said power source in such a manner that each of said phase-shifting device shifts the phase of a first signal propagating through said pole and the phase of a second signal propagating through the other pole such that the shifted phases of both signals will be essentially identical, and such that the shifted signals are added with essentially the same phase, when both poles are connected together to form a single wire through which the resulting added signal propagates

d. a two-polar load, wherein the single wire is split before the load into two lines, with one of the lines connected to one pole of the load directly to transmit a current to the one pole of the load, while the other of the lines is connected to the load via a phase-shifting device that shifts a phase of another current relative to a phase of the one current and transmits another current with the shifted phase to the load.

2. A single-wire electric transmission line system according to claim 1, in which the phase-shifting device is an inverter that shifts the phase of its corresponding pole by +90 degrees, by −90 degrees, or by 180 degrees, such that the shifted signal is added with essentially the same phase.

3. A system according to claim 1, in which the phase-shifting device is a transformer with opposite windings.

4. A system according to claim 1, in which the phase-shifting device is a half-period delay line with respect to the length of the line that is connected to the other pole of the source.

5. A system according to claim 4, in which the delay line is a one-port strip line including metal wire on dielectric, which delay line lying on the metallic padding.

6. 6. A system according to claim 1, in which the phase-shifting device is a digital module adapted for performing a phase shifting.

7. 7. A system according to claim 6, in which the digital module is a Hilbert transform device.

Patent US6297971B1

US patent 10,250,661P6 B1 System for charging electrically driven vehicles with a single line.

US *Patent* No. 10305289. Phase converter for vector conversion of three-phase signals November 20, 2017

A phase converter for electrical signals is configured for obtaining a vector sum of phase signals or subdividing one signal into several phase signals, including transformers, and configured for successive addition of signals received from secondary windings of the transformers and inversion of one or several of the signals, or for subdivision of one signal into several phase signals.

Description

Background of the Invention

The present invention relates in general to phase converters in electrical systems for transmission of electrical energy.

A phase converter was first disclosed in US Pat. No. US427, 978 of Dolivo-Dobrowolsky, which deals with a method of obtaining a three-phase electric signal in an electrical system.

Many frequency-based methods for conversion of a single-phase electric signal into a three-phase electric signal via a permanent current with the use of converters are known. All of them, however, involve significant electrical power losses.

It is known to convert electrical signals by converters for their transmission through one wire or several wires, which are disclosed, for example, in single-wire electrical energy transmission by Nikola Tesla (US Pat. No. 1,119,736). The Goubau line, a single-wire transmission line at microwave frequencies. (Geog Goubau, "Surface Waves and Their Application to Transmission Lines," *Journal of Applied Physics* 21 (1950); AFEP experiment based on the Russian patent application by S. and K. Avramenko (PCT/GB93100960). In these converters, the phases of the signals do not actually change, but their frequency increases or their shape changes from AC to DC.

These methods that use known converters have substantial disadvantages in that they are expensive to build and install, the parameters of resulting signals depend on changes of a load, and the systems that use these methods are not reversible.

US Pat. Nos. 9,608,441and 9,246,405 disclose methods for the conversion of one-phase or three-phase signals to provide a single-line system. In these methods, the phases of input signals are made identical by means of phase shifters, and then they are added to each other. A disadvantage of these methods is dependence of phases of shifts from resistances of loads. The values of these resistances can vary in the process of use of the systems.

Summary of the Invention

Accordingly, it is an object of the present invention to provide a phase convertor that when used in systems for transmission of electrical energy eliminates the above-specified disadvantages.

In keeping with these objects and with others that will become apparent hereinafter, one feature of the present invention resides, briefly stated, in a phase converter for electrical signals, which comprises means for obtaining a vector sum of phase signals, including transformers, and configured for successive addition of signals received from secondary windings of the transformers and inversion of one or several of the signals.

According to a further feature of the present invention, the secondary windings of the transformers are connected in series, the primary windings of the transformers receive signals of all phases, one of the signals is preliminarily inverted by a transformer with windings that are connected opposite with one another, one of the ends of a connection of the secondary winding forms an outlet of the converter, and its second end is connected to a nullifier.

According to a further feature of the present invention, the abovementioned means include an additional transformer with a winding connected between the outlet of the converter and the nullifier, and both ends of the secondary winding form an outlet.

According to a further feature of the present invention, a single signal, which is vector V, is supplied to an input of the converter. The single signal is divided into three signals: A, B, and C. Signal A is obtained by turning a phase of the vector V by 60° by a capacitor or an inductance winding whose reactive resistance is greater than a reactive resistance of a load of the converter. Signal B is obtained by inverting a copy of the vector V. Signal C is obtained by a vector addition of copies of signals A and B.

According to a further feature of the present invention, a transformer is connected at the input of the converter, and its winding is connected to an output of a single phase line, while its secondary winding is connected between an input of the inverter and a nullifier.

When the converter is designed according to the present invention, it eliminates the disadvantages of the prior art and provides highly advantageous results.

The novel features of the present invention are set forth in particular in the appended claims.

The invention itself, both as to its construction and its method of operation will be best understood from the following description of preferred embodiments that is accompanied by the following drawings.

Brief Description of the Drawings

Figure 1 is a view symbolically showing a converter according to the invention for converting a three-phase signal into a single-phase signal.

Figure 2 is a view symbolically showing a converter according to the invention for converting a single-wire signal into a three-phase signal.

Figure 4 is a view symbolically showing a converter according to the invention for converting a single-phase signal into a three-phase signal.

Figure 5 is a view showing vectors of a three-phase signal according to the present invention.

Figure 6 is a view showing inverting of a vector **3** by the convertor according to the present invention.

Figure 7 is a view showing currents produced by two vectors 1 and 2 separately by the convertor according to the present invention.

Figure 8 is a view showing currents produced by two vectors 1 and 2 together by the convertor according to the present invention.

Figure 9 is a view showing an electrical scheme of a converter C3-1 according to the present invention.

Figure 10 is a view showing an electrical scheme of a converter C3-2 according to the present invention.

Figure 11 is a view showing a vector synthesis of a converter C3-1 with the use of a capacitor according to the present invention.

Figure 12 is a view showing an electrical scheme of a converter C1-3 with the use of a capacitor according to the present invention.

Figure 13 is a view showing a vector synthesis of a converter C3-1 with the use of an inductance according to the present invention.

Figure 14 is a view showing an electrical scheme of a converter C1-3 with the use of an inductance according to the present invention.

Figure 15 is a view showing a simulation of the operation of the converter C3-1 and results of the simulation according to the present invention.

Figure 16 is a view showing a simulation of the operation of the converters C3-1 with C1-3 including step-up and step-down transformers and results of the simulation according to the present invention.

Description of the Preferred Embodiments

The converter according to the present invention is designed to operate on the basis of a vector synthesis.

It is known that in a three-phase electrical energy transmission system, the electrical energy is transmitted through three lines or wires, and phases of electrical signals are offset from each other by 120°. To obtain a single-phase signal, the three-phase signal is separated into three signals, and they are used for different loads.

It is, however, sometimes necessary to convert the whole three-phase signal into one single-phase signal (two-wire signal). For example, it takes place when it is required to supply the whole power supplied from the three-phase system to one single-phase load. This is not possible to achieve by simple summation of the three signals because a sum of the three signals that are offset from each other by 120° is equal to zero.

The converter according to the present invention is configured so that it makes possible a conversion of a three-phase signal into a single-phase (two-wire) signal, or into a single-wire signal, and vice versa.

The convertor according to the present invention for converting a three-phase signal into a single wire signal is symbolically shown in Figure 1.

The convertor according to the present invention for converting a single-wire signal into a three-phase is symbolically shown in Figure 2.

The convertor according to the present invention for converting a three-phase signal into a single-phase signal is symbolically shown in Figure 3.

The convertor according to the present invention for converting a single-phase signal into a three-phase signal is symbolically shown in Figure 4.

The convertor according to the present invention for converting a three-phase signal into a single wire signal is symbolically shown in Figure 1, which is designed, for example, as follows. It is known that the phases of signals or currents in a three-phase system are offset from each other by 120°, as shown in Figure 5.

For obtaining from the three-phase signal of one single-line or single-wire signal, the direction of a vector of one of the currents is changed to an opposite direction, for example, that of vector **3**. As a result, the angles of all vectors are obtained, as shown in Figure 6. Then all three vectors are summated.

It is shown below that when the converter according to the present invention uses the above-described method, which is carried out by, it will not lead to any losses.

For a three-phase system, the following is known:

1. A sum of three signals in a three-phase system is equal to zero.
2. It is known that the power of a balanced three-phase system is equal to the sum of the powers of three phases.

Let us summate two vectors of voltages (1 and 2) with phases offset by 120°:

$V\Sigma^2 = V1^2 + V2^2 + 2V1^*V2 \ Cos \ (\Delta\varphi)$

$Cos \ 120° = -0.5 \ Cos \ 60° = 0.5$

For $V1 = V2 = V$ and $\Delta\varphi = 120°$

$V\Sigma^2 = V^2 + V^2 - V^*V = V^2$

It can be seen that the value of the summated vector is equal to the value of each of the vectors V. There were two signals with phases + and −60° and voltages of the source V. They were united, and this means that a signal is obtained with a phase equal to 0 and voltage V.

Figure 7 shows the currents that are produced by two vectors 1 and 2 separately, while Figure 8 shows the summated power after uniting the two vectors. In other words, the summated voltage after uniting the two vectors 1 and 2 is equal to 2 V. The value of the sum of the two vectors of voltages is equal to V. This means that the sums of three vectors in Figure 5 will be equal to 0. The power of the three phases will be equal to 3VI, since the current in the common wire will be equal to the triple-phase current. This means that both conditions of a three-phase system are satisfied.

Figure 9 shows a converter C1-3 according to the present invention, which realizes the summation of all three vectors. The three-phase source **9.1** gives the energy to two transformers **9.2** and **9.3**. A transformer **9.3** is introduced, with the use of an opposite connection of the windings, which actually corresponds to the nullifiers of the inventor. The secondary windings of all three transformers are connected in series for the addition of all three vectors.

As can be seen from Figure 9, there are no phase shifters of the types LR or CR. There are only transformers that do not change the power of the signals.

This means that the operation of the converter **3-1** does not depend on changes of load values.

The converter C**3-2** in Figure 10 can be made by connecting to the converter **3-1** of an additional transformer.

The converter C1-3, which uses a capacitor, uses the concept of vector synthesis according to the present invention for the conversion of a single-line or single-wire signal into a three-phase signal in a manner particularly illustrated in Figure 11 of the drawing.

Vector V is supplied to the input of the converter C1-3, and it converts vector V into vectors A, B, C having phase shifts between them of 120°. Vector A (**11.3**) is obtained by turning a phase of a copy of vector V by 60° by means of a capacitor, whose reactive resistance is greater than the active resistance of a load of the converter. Vector B (**11.2**) is obtained as a result of the inversion of vector V. Vector C (**11.1**) is obtained by a vector addition of copies of vectors A and B (**11.3**).

Figure 12 shows an electrical scheme of the converter C1-3 with the use of a capacitor **12.1**. It includes transformers **12.2**, **12.3**, **12.4**, and **12.5**. The transformer **12.3** is introduced into the system with the opposite windings **12.4**, **12.5**, and **12.6** of the loads of the three-phase system A, B, and C. The current in the transformer **12.5** is a vector sum of currents of the load C and B after the inversion and the input current after inversion. The current in the load B is an inverted current of the input signal. Element **12.1** is a capacitor whose reactive resistance is greater than the active resistance of the load C.

The converter C1-3, which uses inductance, uses the concept of vector synthesis according to the present invention for the conversion of a single-line or single-wire signal into a three-shape signal in a manner particularly illustrated in Figure 13 of the drawing. Vector V is supplied to the input of the converter C1-3, and it converts vector V into vectors A, B, and C having phase shifts between them of 120°. Vector A (**13.1**) is obtained by turning a phase of a copy of vector V by 60° by means of an inductance, whose reactive resistance is greater than the active resistance of a load of the converter. Vector B (**13.2**) is obtained as a result of the inversion of the vector V. Vector C (**13.3**) is obtained by a vector addition of copies of vectors A and B.

Figure 14 shows an electrical scheme of the converter C1-3 with the use of an inductor **14.5**. It includes transformers **14.1**, **14.2**, **13.3**, and **14.4**. The transformer **14.1** is introduced into the system with the opposite windings. The current in the transformer **12.4** is a vector sum of currents of the loads A and B after the inversion. The current in the load B is an inverted current of the input signal. Element **14.51** is an inductor whose reactive resistance is greater than the active resistance of the load.

The converter C3-1 can be realized as is shown by stimulation according to the program ADC in Figure 15. It includes the same elements as in Figure 10 but in a form required for stimulation.

The simulation results in Figure 15 show that the sum of the powers of the three phases at the converter input is equal to the signal power on the load. That is, in the case of ideal transformers, this converter operates without loss.

Figure 16 shows a scheme and results of the simulation of the connection of two converters C3-1 and C1-3. Increasing and reducing transformers are introduced between them in the single-wire line.

The values of currents and input data show that the powers supplied from the three-phase source are equal to the powers on the loads.

As a zeroing unit or a ground, it is recommended to use a nullifier. If the resistance of the nullifier is close to zero, then the currents entering it will not cause energy losses. The resistance of the nullifier can be of any low value if several nullifiers connected in parallel are utilized. In this case, a current from the nullifier does not propagate into the ground.

The construction and the operation of the nullifier are disclosed in M. Bank *It Is Quite Another Electricity*, second edition, revised, Partridge Publishing, 2017. The present invention is not limited to the details shown since various modifications and structural changes are possible without departing from the spirit of the invention. What is desired to be protected by Letters Patent is set forth in the appended claims.

Claims

1. A phase converter for electrical signals, comprising means for obtaining a vector sum of phase signals or subdividing one signal into several phase signals, said means including transformers

configured for successive addition of signals received from secondary windings of the transformers and inversion of one or several of the signals, or for subdivision of one signal into several phase signals, where in one or in several of the transformers a secondary winding is switched opposite to its prime winding forming an inverted signal, and in said one or several transformers in which the secondary winding is switched opposite to the prime winding forming the inverted signal the secondary winding and the primary winding have a common point connected to a nullifier or a grounding, while the secondary windings of some of the transformers are connected in series.

2. A phase converter for the electrical signals of claim 1, wherein said means include an additional transformer with a primary winding connected between an outlet of the converter and the nullifier or the grounding and a secondary winding with both ends representing the outlet of the converter.

3. A phase converter for electrical signals, comprising means for obtaining a vector sum of phase signals or subdividing one signal into several phase signals, said means including transformers configured for successive addition of signals received from secondary windings of the transformers and inversion of one or several of the signals, or for subdivision of one signal into several phase signals, where in one or in several of the transformers a secondary winding is switched opposite to its first winding forming an inverted signal, while the secondary windings of some of the transformers are connected in series, further comprising an input, wherein a single signal, which is vector V, is supplied to the input of the converter. The single signal is divided into three signals including first, second, and third. The first vector is

obtained by turning a phase of the sector V by 60° by a capacitor or an inductance winding whose reactive resistance is greater than a reactive resistance of a load of the converter. The second vector is obtained by inverting a copy of the vector V. The third vector is obtained by a vector addition of copies of the first and second vectors.

Charging a One-Wire System

US patent 10,250,661.System for charging electrically driven vehicles with a single line.

Electrical energy transmission system which does not require reservation

Patent number: 11258268

Wideband Omni-directional antenna

Patent number: 10381744

Abstract: System and method for reduction of exposure to electromagnetic radiation emitted while using a communication network, wherein said electromagnetic radiation can potentially cause vulnerabilities to the human body or to the data integrity conveyed thereby by the trans-locating and buffering of a transceiver electromagnetic radiation signal by using an intermediary relay system or method.

Type: Application
Filed: September 7, 2020

Publication date: September 22, 2022
Inventors: Michael Bank, Carmi Halachmi, Eugene Shubov

<u>Electrical energy transmission system that does not require reservation</u>

Patent number: 11258268

Abstract: An electric energy transmission system that does not need a reservation has a generator generating a multiphase electric current, a converter converting it into another electric current, an electric current network connected with the converter and having a first group of electric current lines extending toward electric current users and a second group of electric current ones electrically connecting the electric current lines of the first group with each other, and a plurality of consumer blocks connected with the network and having users that use different electric currents and further converters converting the electric current transmitted by the network into the different electric currents and supplying the different electric currents to the electric current users.

Type: Grant
Filed: May 11, 2021
Date of Patent: February 22, 2022
Inventor: Michael Bank

<u>Wideband omni-directional antenna</u>

Patent number: 10381744

Abstract: A wideband Omni-directional antenna, in which the radiation parameters automatically correspond to the frequency of the emitted signal. It can be made by printing and used in small-size transducers, for example, in cellular telephones. The antenna radiator is formed as an electrically conductive plate, which has a shape of a nonrectangular triangle having two lateral sides of different lengths with first ends of the lateral sides connected with one another in a point connectable to an electric signal source and other opposite second ends, and the electrically conductive plate also has a side that is opposite to the point connectable to the electric signal source and connects the opposite second ends of the lateral sides with each other, thus forming a third side of the triangle of the nonrectangular triangle. The antenna can be built by using two joined triangles.

Type: Grant
Filed: December 7, 2018
Date of Patent: August 13, 2019
Inventor: Michael Bank

Phase converter for vector conversion of three-phase signals

Patent number: 10305289

Abstract: A phase converter for electrical signals is configured for obtaining a vector sum of phase signals or subdividing one signal into several phase signals, including transformers, and configured for successive addition of signals received from the secondary windings of the transformers and inversion of one or several of the signals, or for subdivision of one signal into several phase signals.

Type: Grant
Filed: November 20, 2017
Date of Patent: May 28, 2019

Inventor: Michael Bank

Phase converter for vector conversion of three-phase signals

Publication number: 20190157875

Abstract: A phase converter for electrical signals is configured for obtaining a vector sum of phase signals or subdividing one signal into several phase signals, including transformers and configured for successive addition of signals received from secondary windings of the transformers and inversion of one or several of the signals, or for subdivision of the one signal into the several phase signals.

Type: Application
Filed: November 20, 2017
Publication date: May 23, 2019
Inventor: Michael Bank

System for charging electrically driven vehicles with a single line for transmitting electric current from a source to a charging station

Patent number: 10250061

Abstract: A system for charging electrically driven vehicles includes a source of three-phase electrical current, a first converter converting the three-phase or one-phase electric current received from the source into a converted electric current, a single electric current transmission line transmitting the converted electric current, a second converter converting the converted signal received through the single line into three-phase electric current or one-phase electric current or direct current, and a plurality of charging stations receiving from the second converter corresponding currents and provided with

charging components for charging electrically driven vehicles with a corresponding one of the received currents.

Type: Grant
Filed: May 8, 2018
Date of Patent: April 2, 2019

Wideband antenna

Patent number: 10050353

Abstract: A wideband antenna has a first radiator formed as an electrical field signal monopole radiator or a helix radiator, and a second radiator formed as an electric field folded dipole radiator or as a magnetic field loop radiator, with the first radiator radiating a signal at a lowest frequency and its odd harmonics and the second radiator radiating a signal at even harmonics of the lowest frequency.

Type: Grant
Filed: December 30, 2016
Date of Patent: August 14, 2018
Inventors: Michael Bank, Motti Haridim

Surface antenna with a single radiation element

Patent number: 9685704

Abstract: A surface antenna with a single radiation element, which comprises (a) a power source with first and second poles and (b) a phase shifting element, inserted to the path of one of the poles of the power source in such a manner that the phase-shifting device shifts the phase of a first signal propagating through said pole such that the shifted phase of the first signal will be essentially identical to the phase of a second signal propagating through the other pole. The shifted first signal is added to the second signal with essentially the same phase of second signal, whenever both poles are connected together to form a singlewire through which the resulting added signal propagates.

Type: Grant
Filed: January 17, 2013
Date of Patent: June 20, 2017
Inventors: Michael Bank, Motti Haridim

Single-wire electric transmission line

    3.1 Wideband Omni-directional antenna
    Patent number: 10381744

    3.2 Phase converter for vector conversion of three-phase signals
    Patent number: 10305289

    3.3 Phase converter for vector conversion of three-phase signals
    Publication number: 20190157875

Classifications

_H02M1/4233_ Arrangements for improving the power factor of AC input using a bridge converter comprising active switches.

US6297971B1

Description

<u>System for charging electrically driven vehicles with a single line for transmitting electric current from a source to a charging station</u>

Patent number: 10250061

Other subsequent patents concerning the single-wire method

Inventor: Michael Bank

<u>Wireless mobile communication system without pilot signals</u>

Patent number: 7986740

Abstract: Method and system for allowing abandoning pilot signals use and for increasing the immunity to Doppler Effect influence in OFDMA-based wireless mobile communication systems and as a result make them more efficient. This is carried out by transmitting N orthogonal I and Q values of symbols, N times on N frequencies, where N is a power of two. To be able to select the desired signal from a mixture of N signals, signs of symbol of each signal vary according to one of N-order Walsh functions.

Type: Grant
Filed: August 10, 2006
Date of Patent: July 26, 2011

Patent <u>SINGLE-WIRE ELECTRIC TRANSMISSION LINE</u>

Publication number: 20140152123

Abstract: A single-wire electric transmission line system that includes a power sources having first and second poles and a phase-shifting device, coupled to one of the poles of the power source, in such a manner that the phase-shifting device shifts the phase of a first signal propagating through the pole such that the shifted phase of the first signal will be essentially identical to the phase of a second signal propagating through the other pole. The shifted first signal is added to the second signal with essentially the same phase of second signal, whenever both poles are connected together to form a single-wire, through which the resulting added signal propagates.

Type: Application
Filed: February 4, 2014
Publication date: June 5, 2014
Inventor: Michael Bank

Wireless mobile communication system without pilot signals

Patent number: 7986740

Abstract: Method and system for allowing abandoning pilot signals use and for increasing the immunity to Doppler effect influence in OFDMA based wireless mobile communication systems and as a result, make them more efficient. This is carried out by transmitting N orthogonal I and Q values of symbols, N times on N frequencies, where N is a power of two. In order to be able to select the desired signal from a mixture of N signals, signs of symbol of each signal vary according to one of N-order Walsh functions.

Type: Grant
Filed: August 10, 2006

Date of Patent: July 26, 2011

Patent US**9608441B2**

Description

CROSS-REFERENCE TO RELATED APPLICATIONS

This application is a Continuation-in-Part of International Application No. PCT/IL2012/000291 filed Aug. 2, 2012, designating the United States and claiming priority to U.S. Provisional Application No. 61/514,906, filed Aug. 4, 2011, the disclosures of both foregoing applications being incorporated herein by reference in their entireties.

FIELD OF THE INVENTION

The present invention relates to the field of electrical system. More particularly, the invention relates to an electrical transmission system which uses only a single-wire electric transmission line while eliminating the need to use the ground or another wire as commonly used as a second line.

BACKGROUND OF THE INVENTION

Usually in books, articles, or lectures authors explain the work of an electrical circuit (A-Line) as the process of current flowing from the generator to the load by one wire, and then back to the generator by another wire. But it is known that free-access electrons move relatively slowly, and the electrical energy is transmitted at light speed. Actually today's wires electric system uses two or more channels (wires) for transmitting energy or information. While in both channels there is the same information. It is known that active (real) power does not return from load to the generator. From this point of view may be does not need second channel in electrical system. In other words may be a line of electric system can be a single wire.

In the prior-art, there were attempts to perform electrical energy transmission by means of one wire. First applications of the single-wire electrical energy transmission were disclosed by Nikola Tesla in U.S. Pat. No 1,119,736 and in British Patent No. 8,200. Another single line transmission technique is known as the Goubau line or G-line for short, which is a type of single-wire transmission line which is used at UHF and microwave frequencies (see Geog Goubau, "Surface waves and their Application to Transmission Lines," Journal of Applied Physics, Volume 21, November, 1950). However, a G-line is a type of waveguide, rather than a wire in an electric circuit. There was experiment based on the Russian patent application 1993 year by Stanislav and Konstantin Avramenko [6-8}. All these proposals are based on signal processing like frequency up converting or signal straightening. These processing influences on transmitting information and lead to power lose.

There is also an electricity distribution method using only one conductor, but with the participation of earth. This method is known as the Single Wire Earth Return (SWER). However, the simplification of the energy transfer in this system is achieved due to the loss of half the power produced by the source.

It is well known advantages of three-phase system where energy transmitted by four wires. The presence of four wires is not the only drawback of three-phase system. Another drawback may be the fact that line voltage between two wires in this system at the root of the three above of phase voltage. This may have negative consequences, given such a corona effect and additional losses in the lines.

It is an object of the present invention to provide an electric system which is capable of using a single-wire channel for transmitting energy or information without signal form changing and additional loses.

It is another object of the present invention to provide an electrical system that does not use the ground instead of the second wire.

Other objects and advantages of the invention will become apparent as the description proceeds.

SUMMARY OF THE INVENTION

The present invention relates to a single-wire electric transmission line system, which comprises:

The present invention further relates to a single-wire electric transmission line system, which comprises two phase-shifting devices, coupled to each of the poles of the power source in such a manner that each of said phase shifting device shifts the phase of a first signal propagating through said pole and the phase of a second signal propagating through the other pole such that the shifted phases of both signals will be essentially identical, and such that the shifted signals are added with essentially the same phase, whenever both poles are connected together to form a single-wire, through which the resulting added signal propagates.

According to an embodiment of the invention, the phase shifting device(s) is an inverter that shifts the phase of its corresponding pole by +90 degrees, −90 degrees or by 180 degrees, such that the shifted signal(s) is added with essentially the same phase.

According to an embodiment of the invention, the phase shifting device is a transformer with opposite windings.

According to an embodiment of the invention, one of the two phase shifting devices is a Low Pass Filter (LPF) and the other phase shifting device is a High Pass Filter (HPF).

According to an embodiment of the invention, the phase shifting device is an essentially half period delay line with respect to the length of the line that is connected to the other pole of the source. For example, the delay line is one-port strip line including metal wire on dielectric, which lying on a metallic padding.

According to an embodiment of the invention, the phase shifting device(s) is a digital module adapted for performing phase shifting. For example, the digital module is a Hilbert transform device.

According to an embodiment of the invention, in the case of a DC signal, the phase shifting device runs as two capacitors connected in turn to charge through the keys to one of the outputs of a bipolar DC power supply, a second end connected to the power of the capacitor is grounded, the end of the capacitor disconnected from the source, who at the time of charging was grounded is connected to another output bipolar DC power supply and to the input of a single-line, the other end of the capacitor is grounded.

According to an embodiment of the invention, the single-wire is connected to a corresponding single-wire load module that includes a two polar load and phase shifting device coupled to one polar of said load, by splitting said single-wire into two lines, such that one line is coupled to said phase shifting device and the other line is coupled to the load, in such a manner that currents are flow in both lines, but in opposite phases with respect to one another.

According to an embodiment of the invention, the single-wire is split into three wires, wherein each of said three wires is connected to a different pole of a three-phase load via a corresponding phase shifting device, in order to form a single-wire three-phase system, in the following manner:

According to an embodiment of the invention, the first phase shifting device of the three-phase system is an inductance resistance and the second phase shifting device of said three-phase system is a capacitor resistance.

In another aspect the invention relates to a single-wire load (instead of ordinary two wires load), which comprises:

BRIEF DESCRIPTION OF THE DRAWINGS

In the drawings:

FIG. 1 schematically illustrates an example of conventional electric system (A-line), according to the prior-art;

FIG. 2 schematically illustrates a single-wire electric system (B-Line) that is equivalent to the A-line system of FIG. 1, according to an embodiment of the present invention;

FIG. 3 is a print out of the simulation results of the B-Line system of FIG. 2;

FIG. 4 schematically illustrates a phase shifting device in form of a transformer, according to an embodiment of the present invention;

FIG. 5 is a print out of the simulation result of a B-Line system with the transformer of FIG. 4;

FIG. 6 schematically illustrates a scheme of B-Line model with dividing transformers;

FIG. 7 schematically illustrates a conventional high frequency long line and its B-Line equivalent implementation;

FIG. 8 the simulation results of the long line and its B-Line equivalent of FIG. 7;

FIG. 9 schematically illustrates an exemplary one-port strip line for frequency of 2.3 GHz;

FIG. 10 is a graph showing the B-Line with the one-port strip line for frequency 2.3 GHz of FIG. 9 and its simulations results;

FIG. 11 schematically illustrates an exemplary implementation of a DC B-Line circuit, according to an embodiment of the present invention;

FIG. 12 schematically illustrates using one-pole source principle, according to an embodiment of the present invention;

FIG. 13 schematically illustrates an exemplary implementation of a B-Line three-phase scheme, according to an embodiment of the present invention;

FIG. 14 is a graph showing the simulation results of the B-Line three-phase scheme of FIG. 13;

FIG. 15 schematically illustrates an exemplary implementation of B-Line three-phase scheme with one pole generators, according to an embodiment of the present invention;

FIG. 16 is a graph showing the simulation results of the B-Line three-phase scheme of FIG. 15; and

FIGS. 17a and 17b schematically illustrate an exemplary implementation of B-Line three-phase scheme with one pole generators and typical three-phase load.

DETAILED DESCRIPTION OF THE INVENTION

Throughout this description the term "B-Line" is used to indicate an electrical circuit as the process of current flowing from the generator to the load by one wire. This term does not imply any particular arrangement or components, and invention is applicable to all suitable configurations of electrical circuits.

First concept—today one can read another explanation as the process of current flowing. Not like from the generator to the load, and then back to the generator. But this explanation is following: "Two potentials derive from two terminal of source with opposite phases to two terminals of load with light speed." So energy flows in one direction.

Second concept—using ground instead of one wire can be for very short distance only; because the earth resistance is much larger than the resistance of copper. According to the resistance of the earth can be from 5 to 5000 ohms per meter. In many electrical systems grounding is used to potential zeroing. An electrical ground system should have an appropriate current-carrying capability to serve as an adequate zero-voltage reference level. In electronic circuit theory, a "ground" is usually idealized as an infinite source or sink for charge, which can absorb an unlimited amount of current without changing its potential. The current flows into the ground and spreads out in an endless ground, as is the case with a protective earth. In the case of protective grounding, if an accident happens, the current anywhere in the other place does not get. The main characteristic of the grounding resistance is spreading current, i.e., a resistance that the earth (ground) has a current spreading at the site of this current. Land spreading is a ground area that surrounds the grounding electrodes, in which the boundary of the current density is so low that potential, which has virtually no land, depends on the current flowing from the electrodes. That is why outside of this boundary current can always be equated to zero. In other words, if one point of scheme connected to ground, it does not mean that the energy or the information is transmitted to another point scheme, which is also connected to ground. Both points have potential equal zero.

Third concept—If one would like to get adequate electrical energy transmitting system processing, one need to do that source and load can "see" the same resistances. And load current mast is the same that is match to Ohm low.

Reference will now be made to several embodiments of the present invention(s), examples of which are illustrated in the accompanying figures. Wherever practicable similar or like reference numbers may be used in the figures and may indicate similar or like functionality. The figures depict embodiments of the present invention for purposes of illustration only. One skilled in the art will readily recognize from the following description that alternative embodiments of the structures and methods illustrated herein may be employed without departing from the principles of the invention described herein.

The terms, "for example," "e.g.," "optionally," as used herein, are intended to be used to introduce non-limiting examples. While certain references are made to certain example system components or services, other components and services can be used as well and/ or the example components can be combined into fewer components and/or divided into further components.

It will be better to explain the main idea of a single-wire electric system of the present invention (i.e., B-Line) by comparison with a conventional electric system (i.e., A-Line). FIGS. 1 and 2 schematically illustrate an A-Line circuit and a B-Line circuit, respectively. Both circuits include a common power source 2 (e.g., 1 volt generator), a load 3 (e.g., R=10 kOhm) and the currents is about 90 microamperes ($I{\approx}90$ μA). At the A-Line circuit the lines resistance is about 1 rOhm, and at the B-Line circuit, the resistance of the single-wire transmission line is about 0.5 KOhm as will be described in further details hereinafter. The equivalent B-Line circuit includes a first phase shifter 1 coupled to one poles of the power source 2 and a second phase shifter coupled to one of the poles of the load 3.

The B-Line system of the present invention is based on the assumption that it would be possible to combine two wires (i.e., the electric lines running out from the first pole and the second pole of a power source) if currents would be of the same amplitudes and same phases. For example, this can be achieved by inserting a phase shifting device (i.e., the phase shifter 1) in one of the lines. The phase shifting device shifts the phase of a first signal propagating through that line such that the shifted phase of the first signal will be essentially identical to the phase of a second signal propagating through the other line. For instance, 10 milliseconds delay line can be used for signal with a frequency of 50 Hz. After the phase shifting device, phases and amplitudes of the currents in both lines are essentially identical. Thus, at the generator side (i.e., at the power source **2** side), both lines can be combined into a single wire, such that the shifted first signal is added to the second signal with essentially the same phase of the second signal, whenever both lines are connected together to form a single-wire, through which the resulting added signal propagates (i.e., the sum of the currents from both lines).

At the load side, the single wire splits into two wires (i.e., two lines), and similarly to the generator side, a phase shifting device (i.e., a second phase shifter **1**) can be inserted before the load **3** in one of the split wires in order to ensure a normal functionality of the load **3**. As a result, the two conventional wire system (FIG. 1) turns into one-way B-Line system (FIG. 2), but the power source **2** and the load **3** will "see" the conventional two wires system (i.e., A-Line).

According to an embodiment of the invention, the needed phase shift can be achieved by means of a phase shifting device in form of a delay line, a transformer with opposite windings, low pass and high pass filters, digital phase shifters such as Hilbert transform device(s), etc. For example, if a delay line is used as a phase shifting device, then its delay must correspond to half period. In the case of 50 or 60 Hz frequencies it is practically impossible using delay line, recall that wire, which corresponds to half wave length, has length equals 3000 or 2500 km. It is convenient on low frequencies to use transformer with opposite windings as phase shifter. As for high frequencies the good solution is delay line.

The main idea of the single-wire electric transmission line of the present invention was supported on ADS and CST simulations programs. Series of simulations with different phase shifters and various resistance lines were carried out. Each simulation was carried out for the A-Line and the B-Line. For clarity, FIGS. 1-3 show the conditions and the simulation results including polarity and magnitude of currents.

That's one of the simulations for the verification of Ohm's law in the proposed scheme (see FIG. 1). In this typical A-Line circuit, current amplitude everywhere should be 90 µA, wherein 0.5 kOhm is the lines resistance.

In the proposed B-Line scheme (see FIG. 2), we added phase two shifting devices the first at the input and the second at the output, and combined the two lines. As a result a line resistance is 0.5 kOhm. The simulation shows that the currents at the input and output have not changed. The polarity of the load current depends on where the phase shifting devices are at the top or bottom.

One can see on FIG. 3 the simulation results of the B-Line system of FIG. 2. For example, in case the phase shifting device is a transformer with opposite windings, then reverse one wire current phase by the transformer can be reset the current flowing from the winding only. Simply connect the windings cannot be, otherwise the current from one winding to another will flow and the transformer will not perform its functions. As in other similar cases, zeroing can be done with earth (see "Circuit Grounds and Grounding Practices,"

George Hunka, Undergraduate Laboratory, Dept. of EE, University of Pennsylvania). As will be shown in the following section, the land is not involved in the transfer of energy from the source to the load.

FIG. 4 schematically illustrates a phase shifting device that can be used in conjunction with the invention. In this embodiment, the phase shifting device is in form of a transformer. The phase shifting device illustrated in this figure is particularly convenient because it can be easily applied to low frequency systems. The phase shifting device is generally indicated by numeral 1 in the figures.

FIG. 5 is print out that shows the results of a B-Line circuit simulation with two units of inverter **1** (as indicated by the transformers TF1 and TF2). The first transformer TF2 is coupled to an AC voltage source SRC **1** (as indicated by numeral 2) and the second transformer TF1 is coupled to the load **3** (as indicated by the resistor RI). One can see on FIG. 5 B-Line circuit with ideal 1:1 transformers simulation.

If the B-Line is used in a system with raising or lowering the voltage, the inverter **1** must be used in both lines. In the one line is used as the transformer with the same included windings (as indicated by transformer TF2) and in the second line with opposite included windings (as indicated by transformer TF1). The grounding in FIG. 5 is zeroing and therefore it is not used and cannot be used as the return path (i.e., the second line). There are several evidences that the earth is not involved in the transfer of power, although one of any evidence would be enough. The main evidence is that the current in B-Line equals to double current in normal scheme and corresponds to Ohm low. So it is impossible any additional current.

Obviously, in the case of a normal two-wire circuit where the source gives 1 V and a load resistance is 50 ohms the current will be equal to 20 mA. For example, in the case of the B-Line circuit like in FIG. 5 the current in wire should be 40 mA.

With the aim of experimental verification of the proposed solutions were prepared a number of models. Details of the layout mounted on a wooden board, as a zeroing-grounding used electrical network protective grounding. All voltages and currents in the model coincided with the results of the simulation. To eliminate possible doubts about the possible involvement of the land in signal transduction through the neutral wire three-phase system was tested model with dividing (isolating) transformer at the input. This model scheme is shown in FIG. 6. The model shown in FIG. 6 continued to operate normally and when it was taken out of the receiving part of the laboratory at a distance of about 80 meter and used as a grounding metal rod.

B-Line on High Frequency

Let us show that B-line idea is correct for the high frequency too. On frequency 50 Hz simulations where made by ADS program. This program allows simulating different elements but not electrical lines. So for electrical lines simulations was used element like delay line. On height frequencies one can implement CST program. This program allows simulating different elements including electrical lines.

First we compare normal long line with characteristic impedance 300 Ohm with B-Line on frequency 1.1 GHz. Both models are shown in FIG. 7, wherein FIG. 8 shows the simulation results of models **1** and **2** of FIG. 7, on frequency of 1 GHz (as indicated by parameters **S11** and **S21**). On 1.1 GHz it was possible to make delay lines by lines with long equals half wave long. Parameter S21 is the same practically. Parameter S11 of model **2** is better than S11 of model **1**. One can see on FIG. 8 on 1.1 GHz S11 of B-Line is −20 dB and of normal long line is −10 dB. This means that in case of B-line all energy goes from source to load (i.e., there is no power loss).

In high frequency it is possible to make delay line like one-port strip line, e.g., as shown with respect to FIG. 9. With this strip line was made simulation of one wire long line. The simulation results in terms of S-parameter (S1 and S2) magnitude (in dB) are shown in the graph of FIG. 10. The matching long the line is infinitely wide band passes (see appendix about eternal resonance system). This is an advantage, but also disadvantages. There is an advantage because you can pass on a long line of multiple signals with different frequencies. However, in a real system there is always some noise. Even if noise is weak, but in an infinitely wide band it will be infinitely large noise (of course, if the noise is white). Of course, you can apply a filter at the input of the receiver. But this is often problematic. The filter introduces loss and increases the noise factor.

The proposed single-wire system (B-Line) is a selective system. The disadvantage of B-Line is a need to change the delay line in case of change of frequency. B-Line is compatible with the source and load, and in this sense no different from the usual long line. It is selective, but rather broadband. It has no requirements of symmetry, which is often a problem in the prior-art systems when using long line inside the apparatus, where can be different influences on each wire.

DC B-Line

To implement the inverter **1** in a DC circuitry it requires a different solution then the aforementioned transformers. According to an embodiment of the invention, it is proposed to use two capacitors and corresponding switches to implement the inverter **1** (as shown with respect to FIG. 11 in the source side **2** and correspondingly at the load side **3**). Each of the inverter **1** operates as follows: In one period the first capacitor is charges and the second is discharged. In second period they switch functions. Charging current is in one direction, but discharging current direction is reversed.

In this embodiment, in line current has one direction, positive or negative. In this figure, the direction is positive. The resistance value is usually set. So first and second period's duration can only be choosing by value of the capacitors. For example, such a DC B-Line system can be implemented in an electrical railway system (i.e., tramway). In this case, it is possible to transmit electrical power only in wire or only in the rails.

One-Pole Source

The idea of B-Line system allows defining another new element of an electrical circuit—one-pole generator (i.e., source). If we will allocate the connection of the generator and the converter in B-Line scheme, we can talk about uni -polar source (as indicated by dotted line in FIG. 12) where one load terminal is connected to a single-wire, and the second load terminal is grounded (connected to zero voltage). In this case there is no loss of energy, as all the current coming from a single line passes through the load.

B-Line Three-Phase Systems

According to some embodiment of the invention, the suggested B-Line concept allows building unbalanced three-phase system where currents in all phases do not depend on loads in another phases. FIG. 13 schematically illustrates a B-Line three-phase scheme with loads 10, 50 and 200 Ohm. Moreover, this B-Line three-phase scheme uses three wires only. The simulation results of this B-Line three-phase scheme are shown in FIG. 15). The simulation results on FIG. 14 show that each current depends only on its load, but not like in common three-phase system.

According to another embodiment of the invention, the B-Line three-phase system can be built without using of inverters in the receiving parts (as shown with respect to FIG. 15 and to its corresponding simulation results as shown in FIG. 16). Actually this scheme uses one pole generators. As one can see in the graph of FIG. 16, the current values are by two times smaller than currents value in scheme with reflectors in receiving parts. But generators currents are smaller by two times too. Therefore there is no power loses in this scheme too. It is possible to combine one-pole source through one wire with normal three-phase load by implementing 1200 phase shifters, as seen in FIGS. 17a–17 b.

According to another embodiment, the single-wire may be split into three wires, where each of the three wires is connected to a different pole of a three-phase load via a corresponding phase shifting device, in order to form a single-wire three-phase system. Accordingly, a first phase shifting device is coupled to one of the poles of the three-phase load in such a manner that the first phase shifting device shifts the phase of a first signal propagating through the pole by +60° (e.g., by using a filter). A second phase shifting device is coupled to the second pole of the three-phase toad in such a manner that the second phase shifting device shifts the phase of a second signal propagating through the second pole by −60° (e.g., by using a filter). A third phase shifting device is coupled to the third pole of the three-phase load in such a manner that the third phase shifting device shifts the phase of a third signal propagating through the third pole by 180° (e.g., by using an inverter). This way, a phase shift of 120° between signals is obtained with minimal energy loss (compared to shifting the phase of the signals by 120° using filters), since the filters are used to shift the phase of the signals only by ±60°.

It should be indicated that if it is desired to protect power lines (cables) there is an option to use a technique where conventional 3 phase high-voltage power lines which extend along a pipe and buried in the ground. However, the high voltage between phases requires substantially separating between them and therefore, the only solution is using 3 insulating pipes (each cable in a separate pipe), to allow sufficient distance between pipes, such that the electric and magnetic field of each line will not induce disturbing currents in the neighboring lines. However, this solution is costly, due to the fact that it is impossible to put all 3 cables in a single pipe. The single-wire electric transmission line system, proposed by the present invention allows using a single high voltage cable (carrying 3 phases) which is extended along a single insulating pipe and buried in the ground, since there are no neighboring lines. This way, the power line is protected against falling trees, rain and falling snow, with relatively low cost, comparing to the need to bury 3 lines.

As will be appreciated by the skilled person the arrangement described in the figures results in an electrical circuit which uses only a single-wire electric transmission line. One-Way system for connection between source and load by one line—(i.e., B-Line) was proposed and checked by simulations and experiments. One way system can be easily implemented as One-pole source, DC B-Line, LF B-Line, HF B-Line, B-Line three-phase system, etc.

It is possible to suppose that using one-way method (i.e., B-Line) can considerable decrease the electrical lines cost. Moreover, B-Line method allows decreasing energy loss in high-voltage electric transmission lines. An additional advantage provided by the invention is that it is possible to achieve decreasing of electrical lines radiation, including Corona effect, so far as one of radiation courses in two lines and three-phase systems have high voltage between lines. Furthermore, B-Line method allows simplifying the high-frequency long lines and improving their options, including easing the requirements for symmetry, good matching and selective properties. Finally, B-Line method also allows building antennas with one radiated element (monopole) equivalent to two element antenna (dipole).

All the above description and examples have been given for the purpose of illustration and are not intended to limit the invention in any way. Many different mechanisms, methods of analysis, electronic and logical elements can be employed, all without exceeding the scope of the invention.

Single-wire electric transmission line

Patent number: 9608441P22

Abstract: A single-wire electric transmission line system that includes a power sources having first and second poles and a phase shifting device, coupled to one of the poles of the power source, in such a manner that the phase shifting device shifts the phase of a first signal propagating through the pole such that the shifted phase of the first signal will be essentially identical to the phase of a second signal propagating through the other pole. The shifted first signal is added to the second signal with essentially the same phase of second signal, whenever both poles are connected together to form a single-wire, through which the resulting added signal propagates.

Claims [7]

Hide Dependent

The invention claimed is:

1. A single-wire electric transmission line system comprising:

    a) A power source having first and second poles; and

    b) a phase shifting device, coupled to one of the poles of said power source so that said phase shifting device shifts the phase of a first signal propagating through said pole and the shifted phase of said first signal will be essentially identical to the phase of a second signal propagating through the other pole, and such that the shifted first signal is added to the second signal with essentially the same phase of second signal, whenever both poles are connected together to form a single-wire, through which the resulting added signal propagates, or:

    c) two phase shifting devices, coupled to each of the poles of said power source in such a manner that each of said phase shifting device shifts the phase of a first signal propagating through said pole and the phase of a second signal propagating through the other pole such that the shifted phases of both signals will be essentially identical, and such that the shifted signals are added with essentially the same phase, when both poles are connected together to form a single-wire, through which the resulting added signal propagates; and

d) a two polar load, wherein the single-wire is split before the load into two lines, with one of the lines connected to one pole of the load directly to transmit a current to the one pole of the load, while the other of the lines is connected to the load via a phase shifting device which shifts a phase of another current relative to a phase of the one current and transmits the another current with the shifted phase to the load.

2. A single-wire electric transmission line system according to claim 1, in which the phase shifting device(s) is an inverter that shifts the phase of its corresponding pole by +90 degrees, −90 degrees or by 180 degrees, such that the shifted signal(s) is added with essentially the same phase.

3. A system according to claim 1, in which the phase shifting device is a transformer with opposite windings.

4. A system according to claim 1, in which the phase shifting device is a half period delay line with respect to the length of the line that is connected to the other pole of the source.

5. A system according to claim 4, in which the delay line is a one-port strip line including metal wire on dielectric, which delay line lying on the metallic padding.

6. A system according to claim 1, in which the phase shifting device(s) is a digital module adapted for performing a phase shifting.

7. A system according to claim 6, in which the digital module is a Hilbert transform device.

Filed: February 4, 2014
Date of Patent: March 28, 2017
Assignee: SLE International LLC

Inventor: Michael Bank

US Patent 9246405B2

Electrical Energy Transmission System with a Single Transmission Line

Abstract

An electrical energy transmission system has a three-phase electric current power source that generates a three-phase electric current having three electric currents, a converting device that converts the three-phase electric current to obtain a common electric current signal formed by the summation of three electric currents having the same phases, and a single-line electrical transmission line that transmits further the thusly produced common electric current signal.

Images (11)

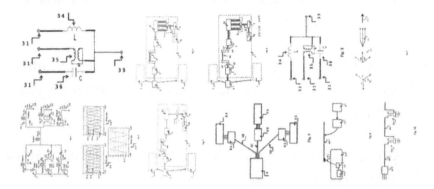

Figures B

Classifications

<u>H02M7/44</u> Conversion of DC power input into AC power output without possibility of reversal by static converters

US9246405B2

United States
Inventor: <u>Michael Bank</u>

Cross-Reference to Related Applications

This application is a continuation-in-part of US patent application Ser. No. 14/172,517 filed August 2, 2012, which is a continuation-in-part of International Application No. PCT/IL2012/000291 filed August 2, 2012, designating the United States and claiming priority to US Provisional Application No. 61/514,906 filed August 4, 2011, the disclosures of all foregoing applications being incorporated herein by reference in their entireties.

Field of the Invention

The present invention relates to the field of electrical systems. More particularly, the invention relates to electrical energy transmission systems that are used to transmit electrical energy generated by three-phase electric power sources over certain distances, including significantly long distances.

Background of the Invention

An electrical energy transmission system for transmitting a generated three-phase current conventionally includes a three-phase electrical power generator and an electrical transmission line that transmits the generated electrical energy to a load.

There were attempts to carry out the electrical energy transmission by means of one wire. First applications of the single-wire electrical energy transmission were disclosed by Nikola Tesla in US Pat. No. 593,138 and in British Patent No. 8,200. Another single-line transmission technique is known as the Goubau line or G-line, which is a type of single-wire transmission line used at UHF and microwave frequencies (see Geog Goubau, "Surface Waves and Their Application to Transmission Lines," *Journal of Applied Physics* 21 (November 1950). However, a G-line is a type of waveguide rather than a wire for an electric circuit. There was also an experiment based on US Pat. No. 6,104,107 by Avramenko et al. All these concepts were based on signal processing, including frequency converting or signal straightening. They, however, negatively influence the process of transmission of electrical energy and lead to loss of power.

Also, an electrical energy distribution method is known with the use of one conductor, however with a return of the electrical current through earth, according to the authors of the proposed method. This method is known as the single-wire earth return (SWER). However, the simplification of the electrical energy transfer in this system is achieved due to the loss of a part of the power produced by the source. One of the reasons for the loss of power is the reactive power caused by the imbalance of the line, and this loss depends on the length of the line.

There are three-phase electrical energy transmission systems that have significant advantages associated with the high efficiency of generators and motors. Conventional three-phase electrical energy transmission systems transmit electrical energy through three or four wires. However, the presence of three or four wires and also of large masts is not the only drawback of these systems. Another drawback is a line voltage between two wires in this system at the root of the three-phase voltage. This may have negative consequences, such as corona effect and additional losses in the lines. An additional disadvantage of the three-phase system is the need to arrange the wires at a distance of several meters from each other. This in turn makes it difficult to use underground lines.

Summary of the Invention

Accordingly, it is an object of the present invention to provide an electrical energy transmission system that transmits electrical energy generated by a three-phase electrical power source and is a further improvement of the existing electrical energy transmission systems of this type.

In keeping with these objects and with others that will become apparent hereinafter, one feature of the present invention resides, briefly stated, in an electrical energy transmission system comprising a three-phase electric current power source generating a three-phase electric current signal including three currents having different phases, a three-phase electric current signal converting device connected with said three-phase electric current source and converting the three-phase electric current signal generated by the latter, and a single-wire electrical energy transmission line connected with said converting device and transmitting further at least a part of the converted three-phase electric current signal.

When the electrical energy transmission system is designed according to the, it allows a transmission of at least a part of the three-phase electric current signal through the single-wire transmission line, which results in significant economy of wires, especially in the systems that carry out transmission of electrical energy generated by three-phase electrical power sources over significant distances.

In accordance with one embodiment of the present invention, the converting device is constructed to shift the phases of at least some of the three electric currents so that the three currents have substantially identical phases in the converted common electrical current signal, which is then transmitted through the single-wire transmission line.

In accordance with a further embodiment of the present invention, a further converting device is provided on the opposite end of the single-wire transmission line and converts the common electric current signal received through the single-wire transmission line by shifting back the phases of at least some of the electric currents into the three-phase electric current signal to be supplied further.

It is also possible in accordance with a still further embodiment of the present invention that the converted common electric current signal transmitted through the single-wire transmission line is not converted back into a three-phase current but instead is supplied through subsequent single-wire transmission lines to consumers.

In accordance with a further embodiment of the present invention, a step-up transformer can be provided before the first-mentioned converting device and a step-down transformer can be provided after the further converting device for correspondingly increasing and reducing a voltage of the electric current signals in order to reduce losses in the wires of the system and connect with the converting devices.

In accordance with still a further embodiment of the present invention, the step-up transformer can be connected by a feedback line with the first-mentioned converting device and/or the step-down transformer can be connected by a feedback line with the second converting device so that the conversions performed by the converting devices, such as shifting of the phases of the electric currents, are carried out with the same desired results, regarding of fluctuations of the electrical resistance of the load, which otherwise would affect the shifting of the phases. In particular, the transformers react to changes in the resistance of the load by generating a control signal for changing their coefficient of transformation to provide a constant output voltage. The control signals for changing the coefficient of transformation are used to change a reactive electrical resistance to maintain a constant ratio of the reactive electrical resistance to the electrical resistance of the load, in order to provide in the converting devices the constant required shifting of phases.

In accordance with an additional embodiment of the present invention, the opposite end of the single-wire transmission line is provided with a further converting device that further transmits three currents of the received common electric current signal through single-wire transmission lines separately to subsequent loads.

In accordance with a further embodiment of the present invention, the currents of the generated three-phase electric signals can be supplied separately through individual single-wire transmission lines to individual consumers.

In accordance with still a further embodiment of the present invention, an electric vehicle can use the transmitted electrical energy so that its electric motor can be connected to the further converting device to receive from the latter the three-phase electric signal through a further single-wire transmission line.

Finally, in accordance with a further embodiment of the invention, the single-wire transmission line can be subdivided into a plurality of line portions, and a plurality of further converting devices convert phases of the currents in the line portions substantially by 180 degrees to provide opposite phases in the neighboring line portions, in order to achieve a sum of energy in the neighboring line portions equal to zero.

The novel features of the present invention are set forth in particular in the appended claims.

The invention itself, both as to its construction and its manner of operation will be best understood from the following description of preferred embodiments, which is accompanied by the following drawings.

Brief Description of the Drawings

Figure 1 is a view schematically showing a conventional system for transmission and distribution of electrical energy generated by a three-phase electric current power source.

Figure 2 is a view schematically showing a system for transmission and distribution of electrical energy generated by a three-phase electric current power source according to a first embodiment of the present invention.

Figure 3 is a view schematically showing a vector diagram of a converting device that converts the corresponding three-phase signal in the electrical energy transmission system according to the present invention.

Figure 4 is a view illustrating a vector diagram illustrating signal conversions by the converting devices of the electrical energy transmission system according to the present invention.

Figure 5 is a view showing a simulation of conversion processes in the scheme of Figure 4, which are carried out in the converting devices of the inventive system.

Figure 6 is a view showing a simulation of corresponding currents that are transmitted through the system for transmission of electrical energy according to the present invention.

Figure 7 is a view schematically showing a system for transmission and distribution of electrical energy generated by a three-phase electric current power source according to a further embodiment of the present invention.

Figure 8 is a view schematically showing a system for transmission and distribution of electrical energy generated by a three-phase electric current power source according to a still further embodiment of the present invention.

Figure 9 is a view schematically showing a system for supplying electric current to an electric train with the use of the electrical energy transmission system according to the present invention.

Figure 10 is a view schematically showing a further embodiment of an electrical transmission line of the electrical energy transmission system according to the present invention.

Detailed Description of the Invention

Figure 1 shows a conventional system for transmission of electrical energy, in particular for transmission of three-phase electric current, for example to some, for example, three large areas 1. The system includes an electric current power source 2 that generates a three-phase electric current signal supplied to a step-up transformer 3 that increases the voltage of the signal. After the step-up transformer, the three-phase electric current signal is transmitted via at least a three- or four-wire air, underground, or underwater line 4 over a required distance. Then the voltage of the transmitted three-phase electric current signal is reduced by a step-down transformer 5 and supplied further for example to a switchgear 6, and then through cable lines 7, a distribution point 8, and a step-down transformer supply center 9 to a residential building 10 or other consumers. As can be seen from Figure 1, the three-phase electric current signal that which includes three currents with phases that are offset from each other by 120′ degrees is transmitted over the required distance and also between all components of the conventional system via at least three-wire lines.

Figure 2 shows a system for transmission of electrical energy, for example, to the three large areas 1, which is constructed in accordance with the present invention. It includes the electric current power source 2 that generates a three-phase electric current signal supplied to the step-up transformer 3 that increases the voltage of the signal. After the step-up transformer, the electric current signal, which includes three electric currents, is transmitted to a converting device 11′. In the converting device 11′, the electric currents of the electric current signal are converted so that their phases are changed and become identical so that all three currents are united into one current to form a common electric current signal. The thusly formed common electric current signal is then transmitted via a single-wire line 4A through a required distance.

After the transmission, in a further converting device 11″, the received electric current signal is converted so that the received electric current signal is divided into three electric currents and their phases are changed so that the phase difference between these three electric current constitutes 120 degrees. The step-down transformer 5 reduces the voltage of the thusly obtained three-phase electric current signal, which can then be supplied to the switchgear 6 and further through the cable lines 7, the distribution point 8, and the step-down transformer supply center 9 to a residential building 10 or other consumers.

The significant difference between the new electrical energy transmission system according to the present invention shown in Figure 2 and the conventional electrical energy train scission system shown in Figure 1 is that in the electrical energy transmission system according to the present invention, the electrical energy or the electrical current signal is transmitted over a required distance between the electrical energy producer and the electrical energy consumer via the single-wire transmission line 4A.

The term "single-wire transmission line" is used to identify such a transmission line that is composed of one wire or of several wires that are twisted with one another and form together effectively as a single electrical conductor.

The electric energy transmission system according to the invention shown in Figure 2 can be provided with feedback lines 12' and 12" associated with the converting devices 11' and 11" correspondingly. This is desirable since an electrical resistance of loads or consumers is not constant and subject to fluctuations, and it can affect the conversion process in the converting device. It is known conventionally that an electrical energy transmission system must supply a constant voltage of an alternating current, since otherwise, damages to equipment can occur. When the electrical parameters of the load—for example, its resistance—change, then in known transformers the actually produced voltage can change correspondingly. These fluctuations of the electrical parameters of the load can also cause changes in the shifting of the phases of the electrical current, and the phases would not be shifted as required in the electrical energy transmission system according to the present invention. The transformers in the system according to the present invention, in response to fluctuations of an electrical resistance of a load, generate a control signal to change their coefficient of transformation in order to maintain constant their output voltage. These control signals to change the coefficient of transformation of the transformers are used to maintain constant a ratio of a reactive resistance to an electrical resistance of the load and to provide in the converting devices the required constant shift of the phases regardless of the fluctuations of the load resistance.

The control signals are supplied through the feedback lines 12′ and 12″ to the converting devices 11′ and 11″. As a result, regardless of the fluctuations in the electrical resistance of the load, the converting devices 11′ and 11″ provide the same consistent results for changing the electric currents in the electric current signals to have identical phases by the converting device 11′ and for changing the electric currents in the electrical current signal to have different phases spaced from each other by 120 degrees by the converting device 11″, correspondingly.

Figure 3 shows an example of realization of the converting device 11′. It includes three lines 31 for supplying three electric currents of a three-phase electric current signal, an inductance 34, an inverter 35, and a capacitor 36; and it is connected to the single-wire line 33, via which the converted electric current signal is transmitted over a required distance. The connection of the inductance and the resistance of the load shifts the phase by minus 60 degrees, the connection of the capacitance with the resistance of the load changes the phase by plus 90 degrees, and the inverter change the phase by 180 degrees.

The converting device 11″ can be composed of the same components as the converting device 11′, but it operates in an opposite way, by converting the incoming common electric current signal with the electric currents having the same phases into the electric current signal in which the phases of the electric currents are spaced from each other by 120 degrees.

Figure 4 shows a vector diagram of a conversion process that takes place in the converting device 11'. Initially in a three-phase electric current signal generated by the electric current power source 2, the electric currents in step 41 have phases that are offset from each other by 120 degrees. The converting device 11' in step 42 shifts the phase of a horizontally illustrated current by 180 degrees and shifts two other currents in step 43 by 60 degrees each to produce a common electric current signal with all currents having the same phases, which in step 44 is supplied into the single-wire transmission line.

Figure 5 shows a scheme of simulation of the conversion that illustrates how the converting device 11' carries out the conversion process. In the left, there are three generators of sine-shaped currents with phases spaced from one another by 120 degrees. Probes or ampere meter 51 shows amplitudes and shapes, or in other words phases of all three currents. Shifting of phases takes place in blocks 34, 35, 36. In block 36, which is a capacitor C, a shift of 60 degrees takes place. In block 35, which is an inverter, the shift of 180 degrees takes place. In block 34, which is an inductance L, a shift of 60 degrees takes place. In the probe 51 in the center, a single sine signal is produced since all currents thatare added to each other must have the same phases. In the right part, a shift of phases takes place in blocks 34, 35, 36. In block 36, which is a capacitor, a shift of 60 degrees takes place. In block 35, which is an inverter, a shift of 120 degrees takes place. In block 35, which is an inductance, a shift of 60 degrees takes place. A three-phase signal is produced. Loads for all currents 52 (resistance

R) are the same and equal to 100 ohms. Knowing R, the values of L and C are received from the following formulas:

$X=arctg\ X/R'$,
where
$X=2\pi FL$
or
$X=1/(2\pi FC)$,
where F is signal frequency, for example, 50 or 60 Hz.

Figure 6 shows a simulation of electric currents that are transmitted through the system according to the present invention. Graph 61 shows currents in ampere meters (probes) in the left part of the diagram of Figure 5. It illustrates that there are three sinusoidal currents with a phase difference of 120 degrees or, in other words, a three-phase signal. Figure 61' shows a single common signal that is produced and ready for transmission through the single-wire line. Figure 61" shows a further three-phase signal that is then produced again. The simulation of Figure 6 shows that the scheme of Figure 5 allows to convert a conventional three-phase signal to a common electrical including three currents with the same phases, and then to convert it back into the three-phase signal.

Figure 7 shows the electrical energy transmission system according to another embodiment of the present invention. In the system shown in Figure 7, the components 2, 3, 11', 4A, and 5–10 correspond to the components of the system shown in Figure 2, which are identified with the same references. However, in the electrical energy transmission system of Figure 7, the electric current signal that has been transmitted via the single-wire transmission line 4A is not converted back into a three-phase electric signal with the electric currents having their phases offset from each other by 120 degrees. Instead, the transmitted electric current signal with three currents having identical phases is supplied further to the subsequent components of the electrical energy transmission system.

Figure 8 shows a further embodiment of the electrical energy transmission system according to the present invention. In this embodiment, the three-phase electric current signal generated by the three-phase electric current source 2 is converted by a converting device 11''' so that here three components from three-phase electric currents are separately and individually supplied through single-wire transmission lines 4B, 4C, 4D further directly to subsequent consumers 81, 82, and 83, and then converted into three-phase currents and transmitted further through additional transmission lines to further consumers 84, 85, 86.

Figure 9 illustrates one of many applications of the electrical energy transmission system according to the present invention, in particular for an electric vehicle, for example, an electric train. The three-phase electrical current power source 2 generates a three-phase electric current signal that is converted by the converting device 11' so that its three currents have the same phases and is then transmitted through the single-wire transmission line 4A. A pantograph 91 of an electric train 92 transmits the electric current signal from the single-wire transmission line 4A to the converting device 11'', which converts the transmitted electric current signal into a three-phase electric current signal with its currents having the phases that are offset from each other by 120 degrees. This three-phase electric current signal is supplied to an electric motor 93 of the electric train 92.

It is also possible to use for the electrical energy supply of an electric vehicle instead of the convertors 11′ and 11″, a convertor that processes a single-phase signal transmitted through a single-wire line and then a convertor thatprocesses the received signal into a one-phase signal supplied to the electric motor of the electric train.

Figure 10 shows a further embodiment of the electrical energy transmission system according to the present invention, in which the single-wire transmission line 4A is subdivided into a plurality of line portions, which for example can have a length of 20–100 km. The line portions are connected with each other via inverters 35A, which can be formed as transformers with the windings that are connected toward each other and zeroing of an intermediate point. They can be similar to the inventors in the converting devices 11 and 11″. It is known that electrical energy transmission lines during current transmission emit energy that causes additional energy losses. In the electrical energy transmission system shown in Figure 10, the converting devices 35A change the phases of the current by 180 degrees so that the currents of each two neighboring line portions 4A have opposite phases. As a result, a sum of the emissions will be equal to zero, and the whole electrical energy transmission line will not emit energy, thus reducing the energy losses.

The present invention is not limited to the details shown since various modifications and structural changes are possible without departing from the spirit of the invention.

What is desired to be protected by Letters Patent is set forth in particular in the appended claims.

Phase Converter

Abstract

A phase converter that converts single-phase AC electric power to balanced three-phase AC power. Two input terminals connected to the output of a single-phase AC power source connect directly to two output terminals of the converter. The phase converter has two serially connected storage capacitors with a common connection, a charging circuit for controlled charging the storage capacitors and an output circuit for controlled discharge of the storage capacitors to provide single -phase AC power to a third output terminal. The charging circuit controls input to the storage capacitor to provide a sinusoidal input current and to step up the voltage to the storage capacitors. The output circuit provides output power to the third output terminal of a predetermined phase and amplitude, relative to the other two output terminals, to result in balanced three-phase AC power at the three output terminals. The phase converter provides a balanced three-phase output for leading power factor, lagging power factor, and resistive loads.

Images (6)

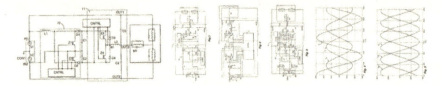

Figures C

Classifications

<u>H02M1/4233</u> Arrangements for improving the power factor of AC input using a bridge converter comprising active switches

<u>US6297971B1</u>

Description

This is a continuation-in-part of Application Ser. No. 09/383,795 filed August 26, 1999, now abandoned. This application claims the benefit under 35 USC § 119(e) of the US provisional patent application no. 60/132,551 filed May 5, 1999.

Technical Field

The present invention relates to faze converters and more particularly to a phase converter for converting single-phase AC power to three-phase AC power.

Background Art

Three-phase AC motors are generally simpler, more reliable, and more efficient than single-phase AC motors. In addition to three-phase AC motors, much high-power industrial equipment requires three-phase AC power. Three-phase AC power is generally supplied to industrial areas. However, only single-phase AC power is available to most residential and rural areas.

The single-phase AC power available in most residential and rural areas is provided by a step-down transformer connected to a high voltage line and, in the United States, is normally supplied as about 240 volts at 60 Hz between the first and second input lines. The transformer is generally center tapped with a neutral line to provide two phases of about 120 volts that are separated by 180 degrees.

Phase converters and inverters convert single-phase AC power to three-phase AC power to power three-phase motors. Phase converters generate a second voltage that is out of phase with the input voltage. The first phase is the voltage between the first and second input line, the second phase is the voltage between the first input line and the second voltage, and the third phase is the voltage between the second input line and the second voltage. Three equal phases spaced 120 degrees apart are provided if the second voltage has an amplitude of (square root over [3/2]) times the amplitude of the input voltage and is 90 degrees out of phase with the input voltage.

The two types of phase converters generally available are the static phase converter and the rotary phase converter. In prior known static phase converters for use with inductive loads, two terminals from the input supply were connected to two of the windings of a three-phase motor, and a capacitor was connected in series between the third winding and one of the terminals from the input supply. The capacitor in combination with the inductive load creates a lead circuit to provide the out-of-phase second voltage.

Such phase converters are disclosed in US Pat. No. 4,492,911 to Molitor, US Pat. No. 4,777,421 to West, US Pat. No. 3,673,480 to Johnstone, and US Pat. No. 5,621,296 to Werner et al. This type of phase converter includes a large capacitor for starting the motor and a smaller capacitor for running the motor. This type of phase converter is relatively inexpensive.However, this type of phase converter can only be used with inductive loads. The capacitor must be selected for the specific inductive load to provide the correct phase shift. Also, the amplitude of the voltage out of the capacitor is at most one-half the input voltage, so this type of phase converter cannot provide balanced currents to the windings at varying loads. Unbalanced currents cause localized heating so that three-phase motors that run with this type of static phase converter can only be run at a fraction of the rated capacity.

US Pat. No. 5,293,108 to Spudich discloses a static phase converter that includes a balancing coil between the two input lines and a capacitor connected between one input line and the third winding to shift the phase. As in the previously described static phase converters, two terminals from the input supply were connected to the first and second windings of a three-phase motor, and a start capacitor and a smaller run capacitor are provided. The balancing coil and capacitor must be selected to match the impedance of the three-phase load with this converter.

Rotary phase converters use motorgenerators powered by single-phase AC power to generate the second voltage signal. Rotary phase converters are disclosed in US Pat. No. 4,656,575 to West, US Pat. No. 5,065,305 to Rich, and US Pat. No. 5,187,654 to Felippe. Rotary phase converters are generally more complex, more expensive, and less efficient than static phase converters and produce an unbalanced output that causes severe imbalances in the phase currents of three-phase motors.

Inverters convert the entire single-phase AC input voltage to a DC voltage with rectifiers and convert the DC voltage into three balanced AC phases with an inverter circuit. Examples of inverters are disclosed in US Pat. No. 4,855,652 to Yamashita et al., US Pat. No. 5,793,623 to Kawashima et al., US Pat. No. 4,849,950 to Sugiura et al., and US Pat. No. 4,978,894 to Takahara. The inverter circuit requires a minimum of six transistors and six diodes as well as control electronics for all of the transistors. Inverters are generally more complex and more expensive than static phase converters. Since the entire single-phase AC input voltage is converted to DC, inverters are inherently less efficient than static phase converters. The output voltage of inverters consists of a pulse-width-modulated (PWM) signal with a high harmonic content, limiting their application to inductive loads. The high-frequency harmonics present in the output voltages cause unwanted reflections in the wires connecting the inverter to the motor load and limit the acceptable distance between the inverter and the motor.

Disclosure of the Invention

A phase converter of the static type for converting single-phase AC power to balanced three-phase power AC is disclosed. The phase converter disclosed includes a charging circuit, first and second storage capacitors, and an output circuit. The charging circuit is connected to an AC power source and includes means for rectifying the positive component of the input voltage and means for stepping up the positive component of the input voltage to charge the first storage capacitor with a positive voltage of about +350V. Means are provided for rectifying the negative component of the input voltage and for stepping up the negative component of the input voltage to charge the second storage capacitor with a negative voltage of about −350V. The charging circuit includes first and second switches that are switched by control electronics at a relatively high frequency with a selected variable duty cycle to provide a sinusoidal input current from the AC power source. The first and second storage capacitors have a common connection that is connected to the AC power source and provide a reference voltage level for the capacitor charging. The output circuit includes first, second, and third output terminals and means, connected to the first and second storage capacitors and to the third output terminal, for providing a selected AC output power signal to the third output terminal from the positive voltage in the first storage capacitor and from the negative voltage in the second storage capacitor. The first output terminal connects to the first input terminal from the AC power source, and the second output terminal connects to the second input terminal from the AC power source.

Brief Description of the Drawings

Details of this invention are described in connection with the accompanying drawings that bear similar reference numerals:

Figure 1 is a schematic circuit diagram of a phase converter embodying the features of the present invention.

Figure 2 is a schematic circuit diagram of another phase converter embodying the features of the present invention.

Figure 3 is a schematic circuit diagram of another phase converter embodying the features of the present invention.

Figure 4 is a graphical representation of the output voltages of the phase converter of the present invention.

Figure 5 is a graphical representation of the relative output voltages of the phase converter of the present invention.

Detailed Description of the Invention

Referring now to Figure 1, the phase converter embodying features of the present invention includes an input connector CON1, a charging circuit 10, first and second storage capacitors C1 and C2, and an output circuit 11. The input connector CON1 is typically a standard 240V plug. The output circuit 11 is connected to a three-phase load, shown as a three-phase motor M1. The input connector CON1 has a first input terminal IN1 for connecting to a first line from a single-phase AC power source and a second input terminal IN2 for connecting to a second input line from a single-phase AC power source.

The charging circuit 10 has a first inductor L1; first and second switches, shown as insulated gate bipolar (IGBT); first and second transistors Z1 and Z2; first and second diodes D1 and D2; and control electronics CNTRL. One end of the first inductor L1 is connected to the first input terminal IN1. The anode of the first diode D1, the cathode of the second diode D2, the collector of the first transistor Z1, and the emitter of the second transistor Z2 all are connected to the other end of the first inductor L1. The emitter of the first transistor Z1 and the collector of the second transistor Z2 are connected to the second input terminal IN2. The control electronics CNTRL is connected to the gates of the first and second transistors Z1 and Z2 and functions to selectively switch the first and second transistors Z1 and Z2 on and off.

The first and second storage capacitors C1 and C2 are serially connected. The end of each of the first and second storage capacitors C1 and C2 that is positively charged by the charging circuit will hereinafter be designated the positive end, and the opposite end will be designated the negative end. Preferably, the first and second storage capacitors C1 and C2 are electrolytic capacitors having positive and negative ends. The positive end of the first storage capacitor C1 is connected to the cathode of the first diode D1, and the negative end of the second storage capacitor C2 is connected to the anode of the second diode D2. The negative end of the first storage capacitor C1 and the positive end of the second storage capacitor C2 have a common connection that is connected to the second input terminal IN2, thereby referencing the common connection to the voltage level at the second input terminal IN2.

In a circuit without the first inductor L1 and the first and second transistors Z1 and Z2, the first diode D1 would feed directly from the first input terminal IN1 to the first storage capacitor C1. Current would only flow from the first input terminal IN1 through the first diode D1 to the first storage capacitor C1 to charge the first storage capacitor C1 when the voltage between the first input terminal IN1 and the second input terminal IN2 was greater than the voltage on the first storage capacitor C1. For an AC source supplying 240 V RMS, the voltage between the first input terminal IN1 and the second input terminal IN2 is $V=\sin \varphi \times 340$. As the voltage on the first storage capacitor C1 approaches the maximum amplitude of the voltage of the AC source, current would flow to the first storage capacitor C1 only during the short period of time each cycle when the amplitude of the voltage of the AC source exceeds the voltage on the first storage capacitor C1. For example, when the first storage capacitor C1 was charged to 330 V, current would flow to the first storage capacitor C1 when $76°<\varphi<104°$, or 16% of the positive portion of each cycle. Since there would be almost no impedance between the first input terminal ·IN1 and the first storage capacitor C1, there would be a large current flow during this short period of time each cycle. Similarly, current would only flow through the second diode D2 to charge the second storage capacitor C2 for the short period of time each cycle when the voltage at the first input terminal IN1 was less or more negative than the voltage at the negative end of the second storage capacitor C2. The current flow into the charging circuit 10 would be highly peaked at the point of maximum voltage, and the capacitor charging would occur only during a small portion of each cycle. Such an input current flow can create problems for power utilities and can distort the input voltages thatare applied across two of the output terminals, as will be described hereinafter.

In the circuit of the present invention, during the portion of each AC cycle in which the voltage at the first input terminal IN1 is positive, the second transistor Z2 is off or open, and the first transistor Z1 is switched on and off at a high frequency with a variable duty cycle. When the first transistor Z1 is on or closed, the first inductor L1 is shorted to the second input terminal IN2, inducing current flow through the first inductor L1. When the first transistor Z1 is off, the current continues to flow due to the inductive action of the first inductor L1. This current flows through the first diode D1 to the positive end of the first storage capacitor C1. Since the current flows to the first storage capacitor C1 even when the voltage at the first input terminal IN1 is less than the voltage at the positive end of the first storage capacitor C1, the combination of the first inductor L1 and the first transistor Z1 can step up the voltage at the positive end of the first storage capacitor C1 to a voltage greater than the maximum voltage at the first input terminal IN1. Similarly, when the voltage at the first input terminal IN1 is negative, the first transistor Z1 is off, and the second transistor Z2 is switched on and off to induce a current flow into the charging circuit to provide sinusoidal input current and to step up the negative voltage at the negative end of the second storage capacitor C2.

The pattern of the variable duty cycle of first and second transistors Z1 and Z2 is selected to provide a sinusoidal input current in phase with the input AC voltage. Preferably, in accordance with the present invention, the first transistor Z1 is switched with a pulse width modulation (PWM) that obeys the equation $D_1 = 1 - |V_1|/V_{C1}$, where V_1 is the instantaneous voltage at the first input terminal IN1, V_{C1} is the voltage at the positive end of the first storage capacitor C1, and D_1, the duty cycle, is the portion of each PWM cycle the first transistor Z1 is on. The PWM frequency f, as an example and not a limitation, can be in the range of about 10 kHz to 100 kHz. Therefore, for the first transistor Z1, the on-time is $t_1 = D_1/f$. Similarly, for the second transistor Z2, the duty cycle is $D_2 = 1 - |V_1|/V_{C2}$ and the on-time is $t_2 = D_2/f$. The sinusoidal input current of the circuit of the present invention prevents distortion of the input voltages and possible problems for power utilities.

The output circuit 11 includes first, second, and third output terminals OUT1, OUT2, and OUT3; third and fourth diodes D3 and D4; third and fourth switches, shown as third and fourth transistors Z3 and Z4; a third inductor L3; third and fourth capacitors C3 and C4; an output node N1; and control electronics CNTRL. The cathode of the third diode D3 and the collector of the third transistor Z3 are connected to the positive end of the first storage capacitor C1, and the anode of the fourth diode D4 and the emitter of the fourth transistor Z4 are connected to the negative end of the second storage capacitor C2. The anode of the third diode D3, the cathode of the fourth diode D4, the emitter of the third transistor Z3, and the collector of the fourth transistor Z4 all are connected to output node N1.

The gates of the third and fourth transistors Z3 and Z4 are connected to the control electronics CNTRL. The control electronics CNTRL switches the third transistor Z3 and the fourth transistor Z4, on and off at a high frequency with a PWM pattern that produces an average voltage sinusoidal waveform. When Z3 is on, Z4 is off and vice versa.

The first output terminal OUT1 is connected directly to the first input terminal IN1, and the second output terminal OUT2 is connected directly to the second input terminal IN2. A third inductor L3 is connected between the output node N1 and the third output terminal OUT3. The third capacitor C3 is connected from the first output terminal OUT1 to the third output terminal OUT3, and the fourth capacitor C4 is connected from the second output terminal OUT2 to the third output terminal OUT3. The first, second, and third output terminals OUT1, OUT2, and OUT3 are shown connected to a three-phase AC electric motor M1. The circuit shown in Figure 1 is suitable for use with inductive, resistive, capacitive, and leading power loads. In a phase converter used only with inductive and resistive loads, node N1 could be connected directly to the third output terminal OUT3, and the second inductor L3 and the third and fourth capacitors C3 and C4 would not be required.

Figure 2 shows a circuit diagram of a phase converter embodying features of the present invention, similar to the circuit diagram of Figure 1, with a modified charging circuit. The emitter of the first transistor Z1 is connected to the negative end of the second storage capacitor C2 instead of to the second input terminal IN2. The collector of the second transistor Z2 is connected to the positive end of the first storage capacitor C1 instead of to the second input terminal IN2. With this circuit, when the voltage across the first and second capacitors C1 and C2 becomes too large, power can be directed back to the first input terminal IN1.

The sequence of operation of the first and second transistors Z1 and Z2 for normal charging of the first and second storage capacitors C1 and C2 is the same as described above for Figure 1, except that during the portion of the cycle when the input voltage is positive, when Z1 is on, the voltage available to force current through L1 is $V_1 + |V_{C2}|$ instead of just V_1. A similar sequence occurs during the negative portion of the cycle when Z2 is on. When the voltage across the first and second capacitors C1 and C2 becomes too large, during the portion of each AC cycle in which the voltage at the first input terminal IN1 is positive, the first transistor Z1 is off or open, and the second transistor Z2 is switched on and off at a high frequency with a variable duty cycle to provide sinusoidal current flow with power flowing from the first storage capacitor C1 to the first input terminal IN1. Similarly, during the portion of each AC cycle in which the voltage at the first input terminal IN1 is negative, the second transistor Z2 is off or open, and the first transistor Z1 is switched on and off at a high frequency with a variable duty cycle so that power flows from the second storage capacitor C2 to the first input terminal IN1.

A first current sensing device, shown as first current sensing transformer CS1, is connected between the first inductor L1 and the common connection of the cathode of the first diode D1, the anode of the second diode D2, the collector of the first transistor Z1, and the emitter of the second transistor Z2. A second current sensing device, shown as second current sensing transformer CS2, is connected between the output node N1 and the third inductor L3. The first and second current sensing transformers CS1 and CS2 connect to the control electronics CNTRL. The control electronics CNTRL monitors the current through the first current sensing transformer CS1, the voltage V_1 at IN1, and the voltages across capacitors C1 and C2 to calculate the PWM duty cycles for the first and second transistors Z1 and Z2 to provide sinusoidal input current. The control electronics CNTRL monitors the current through the second current sensing transformer CS2, the voltage at OUT3, and the voltages across capacitors C1 and C2 to calculate the PWM duty cycles for the third and fourth transistors Z3 and Z4 to provide the proper phase sinusoidal output signal.

Figure 3 shows a phase converter, similar to the phase converter of Figure 1, with a modified charging circuit 10 and a modified output circuit 11. The input connector CON1 has a first input terminal IN1 for connecting to a first line from a single-phase AC power source, a second input terminal IN2 for connecting to a second line from a single-phase AC power source, and a third input terminal IN3 for connection to a neutral line.

The charging circuit 10 has first and second inductors L1 and L2; first and second switches, shown as IGBT; first and second transistors Z1 and Z2; first and second, fifth, sixth, seventh, and eighth diodes D1, D2, D5, D6, D7, and D8; and control electronics CNTRL. The anode of the fifth diode D5 is connected to the first input terminal IN1, and the anode of the sixth diode D6 is connected to the second input terminal IN2. One end of the first inductor L1 connects to the cathodes of the fifth and sixth diodes D5 and D6. The anode of the first diode D1 and the collector of the first transistor Z1 are connected to the other end of the first inductor L1.

The cathode of the seventh diode D7 is connected to the first input terminal IN1, and the cathode of the eighth diode D8 is connected to the second input terminal IN2. One end of the second inductor L2 connects to the anodes of the seventh and eighth diodes D7 and D8. The cathode of the second diode D2 and the emitter of the second transistor Z2 are connected to the other end of the second inductor L2.

The emitter of the first transistor Z1 and the collector of the second transistor Z2 are connected to the third input terminal IN3. The control electronics CNTRL is connected to the gates of the first and second transistors Z1 and Z2 to switch the first and second transistors Z1 and Z2 on and off. The first and second inductors L1 and L2 can be on a single core, as shown, or on separate cores.

The positive end of the first storage capacitor C1 is connected to the cathode of the first diode D1, and the negative end of the second storage capacitor C2 is connected to the anode of the second diode D2. The negative end of the first storage capacitor C1 and the positive end of the second storage capacitor C2 have a common connection that is connected to the third input terminal IN3, thereby referencing the common connection of the first and second storage capacitor C1 and C2 to the voltage level of the neutral input line.

This charging circuit 10 provides full-wave rectification of the input power, whereas the circuit shown in Figures 1 and 2 provide half-wave rectification so that more power is provided for each AC cycle. Full-wave charging reduces the ripple voltage across the first and second storage capacitors C1 and C2. This circuit requires more voltage boost from the step-up arrangement of the inductors and transistors and more components than the half-wave circuits. This circuit also requires connecting to a neutral input line. The full-wave circuit is more suitable for higher power applications, and the half-wave circuits are more suitable for lower power, lower cost applications.

The output circuit 11 includes first, second, and third output terminals OUT1, OUT2, and OUT3; third, fourth, ninth, and tenth diodes D3, D4, D, and D10; third, fourth, fifth, and sixth switches, shown as third, fourth, fifth, and sixth transistors Z3, Z4, Z5, and Z6; a third inductor L3; third and fourth capacitors C3 and C4; an output node N1; and control electronics CNTRL. The cathode of the third diode D3 and the collector of the third transistor Z3 are connected to the positive end of the first storage capacitor C1, and the anode of the fourth diode D4 and the emitter of the fourth transistor Z4 are connected to the negative end of the second storage capacitor C2. The anode of the third diode D3, the cathode of the fourth diode D4, the emitter of the third transistor Z3, and the collector of the fourth transistor Z4 all are connected to output node N1.

The cathode of the ninth diode D9 and the anode of the tenth diode D10 are connected to the output node N1. The emitter of the fifth transistor Z5 is connected to the anode of the ninth diode D9, and the collector of the fifth transistor Z5 is connected to the third input terminal IN3. The collector of the sixth transistor Z6 is connected to the cathode of the tenth diode D10 and the emitter of the sixth transistor Z6 is connected to the third input terminal IN3.

The gates of the third, fourth, fifth, and sixth transistors Z3, Z4, Z5, and Z6 are connected to the control electronics CNTRL. The control electronics CNTRL switches the fifth transistor Z5 on and the third transistor Z3 on and off at a high frequency during the positive portion of each output cycle with a PWM pattern that produces an average voltage sinusoidal positive half wave, and switches the sixth transistor Z6 on and the fourth transistor Z4 on and off at a high frequency during the negative portion of each output cycle with a PWM pattern that produces an average voltage sinusoidal negative half wave. The fifth and sixth transistors Z5 and Z6, with the ninth and tenth diodes D9 and D10, reduce the high-frequency harmonics in the output waveform.

Figure 4 shows the voltages V_1, V_2, and V_3 at the first, second, and third output terminals OUT1, OUT2, and OUT3, respectively, over a period of about 30 milliseconds. The voltages V_1 and V_2 are about 120 VRMS with a maximum amplitude of 120×{square root over (2)}=170V and are 180 degrees out of phase. The maximum amplitude of voltage V_3 is 170×{square root over (3)}=294V and voltage V_3 is 90 degrees out phase with V_1 and V_2. Figure 5 shows these same voltages as the voltages V_{32}, V_{13}, and V_{21} between the first, second, and third output terminals OUT1, OUT2, and OUT3. In this way, by increasing the amplitude of the voltage at the third output terminal OUT3 and shifting the phase by 90 degrees, balanced three-phase AC power is produced by the converter and supplied to the load. The static phase converter of the present invention, unlike many prior known devices, does not require that the components be selected to match a specific load and provides balanced three-phase AC power over a range of loads. This static phase converter is more efficient, less complex, and less expensive than prior known inverters. This phase converter provides sinusoidal input current instead of highly peaked input current, preventing negative effects on the power grid. This phase converter can be used to supply power to inductive, capacitive, or resistive loads.

Although the present invention has been described with a certain degree of particularity, it is understood that the present disclosure has been made by way of example and that changes in details of structure may be made without departing from the spirit thereof.

3.4 System for charging electrically driven vehicles with a single line for transmitting electric current from a source to a charging station

Patent number: 10250061P29

System for charging electrically driven vehicles with a single line for transmitting electric current from a source to a charging station

Abstract

A system for charging electrically driven vehicles includes a source of three-phase electrical current, a first converter converting the three-phase or one-phase electric current received from the source into a converted electric current, a single electric current transmission line transmitting the converted electric current, a second converter converting the converted signal received through the single line into three-phase electric current, or one phase electric current, or direct current, and a plurality of charging stations receiving from the second converter corresponding currents and provided with

charging components for charging electrically driven vehicles with a corresponding one of the received currents.

Images

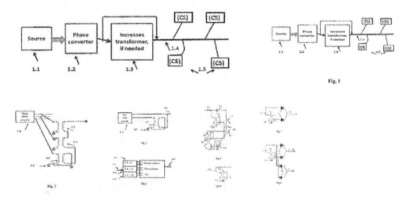

Figures D

Classifications

H02J7/02 Circuit arrangements for charging or depolarizing batteries or for supplying loads from batteries for charging batteries from AC mains by converters

9246405B2

US10250061B1

United States

Background of the Invention

The present invention relates to systems for charging electrically driven vehicles.

Systems for charging electrically driven vehicles are generally known in the modern automotive industry. A known system for charging electrically driven vehicles usually includes a source of electric current, multiple wire lines extending above the ground from the source of electric current, and multiple charging stations connected with the source of electric current by the multiple wire lines for receiving the electric current and provided with charging means for charging electrically driven vehicles with the thusly received current.

Nowadays, however, there is a problem associated with the need for fast charging of electrically driven vehicles. The time of charging depends on voltage in a charging device. The higher the voltage, the shorter the charging time. In residential areas, the voltage is 380 volts, and with this voltage, the time of charging is approximately 8 hours. This is generally acceptable in living areas or in employment areas. However, there are situations when it is necessary to provide a fast charging, for example, on highways or other places where a vehicle battery discharged. It is very expensive to erect high poles with high-voltage wires along highways and in many cases is just impossible.

It is believed that the existing systems for charging electrically driven vehicles can be improved in these aspects.

Summary of the Invention

Accordingly, it is an object of the present invention to provide a system for fast charging electrically driven vehicles, which is a further improvement of existing systems for charging electrically driven vehicles, including those installed on the highway.

In keeping with these objects and with others that will become apparent hereinafter, one feature of the present invention resides, briefly stated, in a system for charging electrically driven vehicles, which has a source of electrical current; first converting means for converting the electric current received from the source into a converted electric current; a single electric current transmission line transmitting the converted electric current; second converting means for converting the converted signal received through the single electric current transmission line into an electric current selected from the group consisting of three-phase electric current, one-phase electric current, direct current, and combinations thereof; a plurality of charging stations connected with the second converting means for receiving from the second converting means one of three-phase electric current, one-phase electric current, direct current, or combinations thereof; and provided with charging means for charging electrically driven vehicle with a corresponding one of the received currents.

When a system for charging electrically driven vehicles is designed in accordance with the present invention, it is significantly advantageous over the existing systems since instead of multiple electrical current transmission lines that are run above the ground, it utilizes a single electrical current transmission line that can be located underground. Also, each charging station can have several different charging currents suitable for charging electric vehicles operating with different types of currents.

It is actually impossible to transmit a three-phase signal underground. It would be necessary to build underground tunnels, since a great distance must be provided between the wires.

According to a further feature of the present invention, the first converting means include a converter for converting a three-phase electric current into an electric signal that can be transmitted through a single electric current transmission line.

According to a further feature of the present invention, the second converting means include a converter for converting the signal received from the single electric current transmission line into a three-phase electric current.

According to a further feature of the present invention, the second converting means include a converter for converting the signal received from the single electric current transmission line into a one-phase electric current.

According to a further feature of the present invention, the second converting means include a converter for converting the signal received from the single electric current transmission line into a direct current.

The novel features of the present invention are set in particular in the appended claims.

The invention itself, however, both as to its construction and manner of operation, will be best understood from the following description of the preferred embodiments, which is accompanied by the following drawings.

Brief Description of the Drawings

Figure 1 is a view showing a system for charging electrically driven vehicles according to the present invention.

Figure 2 is a view showing a converter for converting a three-phase electric current into an electric signal that can be transmitted through a single electric current transmission line.

Figure 3 is a view showing a converter for converting a one-phase electric current into an electric signal that can be transmitted through a single-current transmission line.

Figure 4 is a view showing a charging station of the inventive system for charging electrically driven vehicles.

Figure 5 is a view showing a converter for converting the signal received from the single electric current transmission line into a three-phase electric current.

Figure 6 is a view showing a converter for converting the signal received from the single electric current transmission line into a one-phase electric current.

Figure 7 is a view showing a converter for converting the signal received from the single electric current transmission line into a direct current.

Figure 8 is a view showing a two-pole converter for converting the signal received from the single electric current transmission line into a direct current.

Description of the Preferred Embodiments

The converter shown in Figure 2 that converts a three-phase electric current into an electric current that can be transmitted through the single electric current transmission line 1.4 includes a system of three transformers 2.1., 2.2, and 2.3. The electric currents of each phase of the source of three-phase electric current 1.1 are supplied to each of the primary windings of the transformers 2.1, 2.2, and 2.3. In the transformer 2.3, the windings are connected opposite to one another for inversion of the current. The secondary windings of all transformers are connected in series. The upper end of the secondary winding of the transformer 2.1 is an output of the converter. The lower end of the primary windings of the transformers 2.1, 2.2, and 2.3 and the lower end of the secondary winding of the transformer 2.3 are connected with a nullifier 2.4. The converter is disclosed in our US patent application Ser. No. 15/732,500 filed November 20, 2017. The nullifier 2.4 reduces an electrical potential of the system and can be formed as a conventional grounding or can be formed as a grounding with a limited ground volume, as disclosed in our US patent application Ser. No. 15/144,330 filed May 2, 2016, and in the book by M. Bank titled *It Is Quite Another Electricity*, second edition, revised, Partridge Publishing 2017, Amazon.com.

The converter shown in Figure 3 converts a current that can be transmitted from the source 3.1 through the single electric current transmission line 1.4. It combines two currents after passing one of the currents through the inverter 2.3.

The charging station 1.5 shown in Figure 4 receives the electric current from the single line 1.4. The charging station can have three, two, or only one output converter. A converter C1-3 4.1 converts the signal received through the single line into a three-phase current. A converter C1-2 4.2 converts the signal received through the single line into a one-phase current. A converter C1-DC 4.3 converts the signal received through the single line into a direct current. All these converters have output units connectable with a charging device 4.4 of an electrically driven vehicle.

The output converter for providing a three-phase output current is shown in Figure 5. It provides separation of the current received through the single line 1.4 into three currents and conversion of their phases into phases that are conventionally used in a three-phase system. The first current passes through a phase shifter composed of a capacitor 5.1 or inductor and resistor, where resistance is a load of one of the phases 5.2. This phase shifter shifts the phase by 60 degrees. This means that the ratio of the inductive or capacitive resistance to an active one must be tangent of 60 degrees, or 1.73. The current from the output of the phase shifter is supplied to 5.2, which is a load of the first phase line. The current from the single line 1.4 also goes through the inverter 5.3 and adds in a secondary winding of the transformer 5.4 with the separated current from the single line through the transformer 5.5. The sum of the currents goes into 5.6, which is a load of a second phase line. The current of the third phase line 5.7 is obtained after inverting the separated current of the single line in the inverter 2.3.

Figure 6 shows an output converter for supplying a one-phase output current. The current supplied through the single line 1.4 is separated into two currents, and one of them is inverted. The inverter 6.1 includes a transformer with oppositely connected windings and a nullifier 2.4 connected with both windings.

Figure 7 shows an output converter for supplying a direct current. It provides separation of one of the currents into two currents and conversion of one of them by the inverter 2.3. Both currents without inverting and after the inverter 2.3 passed through diode 7.1

connected with the same polarity. The output points of both diodes are connected and represent an output of a signal DC 7.2.

Figure 8 shows a two-pole output inverter for supplying a direct current. It separates the current received from the single line into two currents, and one of them is inverted by the inverter 2.3. Both currents without inverting and after the inverter 2.3 passed twice through diode 7.1 with one polarity and diode 8.1 connected with another polarity. The output points of both diode pairs are connected and form a two-polar output of the signal DC 7.2 and 8.2.

The present invention is not limited to the details shown since various modifications and structural changes are possible without departing from the spirit of the invention.

What is desired to be protected by Letters Patent is set forth in particular in the appended claims.

Claims [7]

Hide Dependent

What are claimed are as follows

1. A system for charging electrically driven vehicles, comprising

   a. a source of electrical current selected from the group consisting of three-phase current and one-phase current;

   b. first converting means for converting the electric current received from the source into a converted electric current;

c. a single electric current transmission line transmitting the converted electric current;

d. second converting means for converting the converted electric current received through the single electric current transmission line into an electric current selected from the group consisting of three-phase electric current, one-phase electric current, and direct current;

e. a plurality of charging stations connected with the second converting means for receiving from the latter at least one of the three-phase electric current, one-phase electric current, and direct current, and provided with charging means for charging electrically driven vehicles with at least one of the currents received from the second converting means.

2. The system of claim 1, wherein the single electrical current transmission line extends in the ground.

3. The system of claim 1, wherein the first converting means include a system of three transformers, with the electric currents of each phase of the source of three-phase electric current supplied to each of the primary windings of the transformers, with a secondary winding of one of the transformers connected opposite to its primary winding for inversion of the current, the secondary windings of the transformers are connected in series, an upper end of the secondary winding of one of the transformers is an output of the converter, and a lower end of the primary windings of one of the transformers and a lower end of the secondary winding of the other of the transformers are connected with a nullifier.

4. The system of claim 1, wherein the second converting means include an output converter for providing a three-phase output current by separation of the current received through the single line into three currents and conversion of their phases into phases that are conventionally used in a three-phase system, such that a first current passes through a phase shifter composed of a capacitor or inductor and a resistor where resistance is a load of one of the phases, the phase shifter shifts the phase by 60 degrees, the current from the output of the phase shifter is supplied which is a load of the first phase line, the current from the single line also goes through an inverter and adds in a secondary winding of the transformer with the separated current from the single line through the transformer, the sum of the currents goes into a load of a second phase line, and the current of the third phase line is obtained after inverting the separated current of the single line in the inverter.

5. The system of claim 1, wherein the second converting means include an output converter for supplying a one-phase output current, such that the current supplied through the single electric current transmission line is separated into two currents and one of them is inverted by an inverter that includes a transformer with oppositely connected windings and a nullifier connected with both windings.

6. The system of claim 1, wherein the second converting means include an output converter for supplying a direct current by providing a separation of one of the currents into two currents and a conversion of one of them by a converter, with both other currents without inverting and after the inverter passing through diodes connected with the same polarity and having the output

points of both diodes connected and representing an output of the converter.

7. The system of claim 1, wherein the second converting means include a two-pole output inverter for supplying a direct current, with it separating the current received from the single electric current transmission line into two currents and inverting one of them by the inverter, with both other currents without inverting and after the inverter passing twice through diodes with one polarity and diodes connected with another polarity, with the output points of both diode pairs connected and forming a two-polar output of the converter.

Inventors: Michael Bank, Boris Hill, Miriam Bank, Hanit Hill Selecter

Номер number: 7986740

System for charging electrically driven vehicles with a single line for transmitting electric current from a source to a charging station

Abstract

A system for charging electrically driven vehicles includes a source of three-phase electrical current, a first converter converting the three-phase or one-phase electric current received from the source into a converted electric current, a single electric current transmission line transmitting the converted electric current, a second converter converting the converted signal received through the single line into three-phase electric current, or one phase electric current, or direct current, and a plurality of charging stations receiving from the second converter corresponding currents and provided with

charging components for charging electrically driven vehicles with a corresponding one of the received currents.

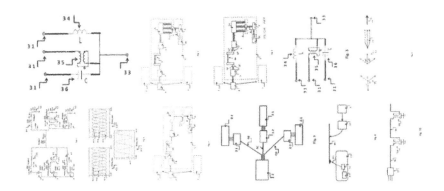

Classifications

H02J7/02 Circuit arrangements for charging or depolarizing batteries or for supplying loads from batteries for charging batteries from ac mains by converters

View 14 more classifications

US10250061B1P32
United States

<u>Download PDF</u> <u>Find Prior Art</u> <u>Similar</u>

Inventor

<u>Michael Bank</u>

Worldwide applications

2018<u>US</u>

Application US15/894,347 events

2018-05-08

Application filed by Michael Bank

2018-05-08

Priority to US15/894,347

2019-04-02

Application granted

2019-04-02

Publication of US**10250061B1**P32

Status

Active

2038-05-08

Anticipated expiration

Description

BACKGROUND OF THE INVENTION

The present invention relates to systems for charging electrically driven vehicles.

System for charging electrically driven vehicles is generally known in the modern automotive industry. A known system for charging electrically driven vehicles usually includes a source of electric current, multiple wires lines extending above the ground from the source of electric current, and multiple charging stations connected with the source of electric current by the multiple wire lines for receiving the electric current and provided with charging means for charging electrically driven vehicles with the thusly received current.

Nowadays however there is a problem associated with the need for fast charging of electrically driven vehicles. The time of charging depends on voltage in a charging device. The higher is the voltage, the shorter is the charging time. In residential areas the voltage is 380 volts, and with this voltage the time of charging is approximately 8 hours. This is generally acceptable in living areas or in employment areas. However, there are situations when it is necessary to provide a fast charging, for example on highways or other places where a vehicle battery discharged. It is very expensive to erect high poles with high voltages wires along highways, and in many cases is just impossible.

It is believed that the existing systems for charging electrically driven vehicles can be improved in these aspects.

SUMMARY OF THE INVENTION

Accordingly, it is an object of the present invention to provide a system for fast charging electrically driven vehicles, which is a further improvement of existing systems for charging electrically driven vehicles, including those installed on the highway.

In keeping with these objects and with others which will become apparent hereinafter one feature of the present invention resides briefly stated in a system for charging electrically driven vehicles, which has a source of electrical current, first converting means for converting the electric current received from the source into a converted electric current, a single electric current transmission line transmitting the converted electric current, second converting means for converting the converted signal received through the single electric current transmission line into an electric current selected from the group consisting of three-phase electric current, one phase electric current, direct current, and combinations thereof, a plurality of charging stations connected with the second converting means for receiving from the second converting means one of three-phase electric current, one phase electric current, direct current, or combinations thereof and provided with charging means for charging electrically driven vehicle with a corresponding one of the received currents.

When a system for charging electrically driven vehicles is designed in accordance with the present invention, it is significantly advantageous over the existing systems since instead of multiple electrical current transmission lines which are run above the ground it utilizes a single electrical current transmission line which can be located underground. Also, each charging station can have several different charging currents suitable for charging electric vehicles operating with different types of currents.

It is actually impossible to transmit a three-phase signal underground. It would be necessary to build underground tunnels, since a great distance must be provided between the wires.

According to a further feature of the present invention the first converting means include a converter for converting a three-phase electric current into an electric signal which can be transmitted through a single electric current transmission line.

According to a further feature of the present invention the second converting means include a converter for converting the signal received from the single electric current transmission line into a three-phase electric current.

According to a further feature of the present invention the second converting means include a converter for converting the signal received from the single electric current transmission line into a one-phase electric current;

According to a further feature of the present invention the second converting means include a converter for converting the signal received from the single electric current transmission line into a direct current.

The novel features of the present invention are set in particular in the appended claims.

The invention itself however both as to its construction and manner of operation will be best understood from the following description of the preferred embodiments, which is accompanied by the following drawings.

BRIEF DESCRIPTION OF THE DRAWINGS

FIG. 1 is a view showing a system for charging electrically driven vehicles according to the present invention;

FIG. 2 is a view showing a converter for converting a three-phase electric current into an electric signal which can be transmitted through a single electric current transmission line;

FIG. 3 is a view showing a converter for converting a one phase electric current into an electric signal which can be transmitted through a single current transmission line;

FIG. 4 is a view showing a charging station of the inventive system for charging electrically driven vehicles;

FIG. 5 is a view showing a converter for converting the signal received from the single electric current transmission line into a three-phase electric current;

FIG. 6 is a view showing a converter for converting the signal received from the single electric current transmission line into a one-phase electric current;

FIG. 7 is a view showing a converter for converting the signal received from the single electric current transmission line into a direct current; and

FIG. 8 is a view showing a two-pole converter for converting the signal received from the single electric current transmission line into a direct current.

DESCRIPTION OF THE PREFERRED EMBODIMENTS

The converter shown in FIG. 2 which converts a three-phase electric current into an electric current which can be transmitted through the single electric current transmission line **1.4** includes a system of three transformers **2.1. 2.2** and **2.3**. Electric currents of each phase of the source of three-phase electric current **1.1** are supplied to each of the primary windings of the transformers **2.1, 2.2, 2.3**. In the transformer **2.3**. the windings are connected opposite to one another for inversion of the current. The secondary windings of all transformers are connected in series. The upper end of the secondary winding of the transformer **2.1** is an output of the converter. The lower end of the primary windings of the transformers **2.1, 2.2** and **2.3** and the lower end of the secondary winding of the transformer **2.3** are connected with a nullifier **2.4**. The converter is disclosed in our U.S. patent application Ser. No. 15/732,500 filed Nov. 20, 2017. The nullifier **2.4** reduces an electrical potential of the system and can be formed as a conventional grounding, or can be formed as a grounding with a limited ground volume, as disclosed in our U.S. patent application Ser. No. 15/144,330 filed May 2, 2016 and in the book MBank "It is Quite Another Electricity," Second Edition, Revised, Partridge Publishing 2017, Amazon.com.

The converter shown in FIG. 3 converts a current which can be transmitted from the source **3.1** through the single electric current transmission line **1.4**. It combines two currents after passing one of the currents through the inverter **2.3**.

The charging station **1.5** shown in FIG. 4 receives the electric current from the single line **1.4**. The charging station can have three, two or only one output converter. A converter C1-3 **4.1** converts the signal received through the single line into a three-phase current. A converter C1-2 **4.2** converts the signal received through the single line into a one phase current. A converter C1-DC **4.3** converts the signal received through the single line into a direct current. All these converters have output units connectable with a charging device **4.4** of an electrically driven vehicle.

The output converter for providing a three-phase output current is shown in FIG. 5. It provides separation of the current received through the single line **1.4** into three currents and conversion of their phases into phases which are conventionally used in a three-phase system. The first current passes through a phase shifter composed of a capacitor **5.1** or inductor and resister, where resistance is a load of one of the phases **5.2**. This phase shifter shifts the phase by 60 degrees. This means that the ratio of the inductive or capacitive resistance to an active one must be tangent of 60 degrees, or 1.73. The current from the output of the phase shifter is supplied to **5.2** which is a load of the first phase line. The current from the single line **1.4** also goes through the inverter **5.3** and adds in a secondary winding of the transformer **5.4** with the separated current from the single line through the transformer **5.5**. The sum of the currents goes into 5.6 which is a load of a second phase line. The current of the third phase line **5.7** is obtained after inverting of the separated current of the single line in the inverter **2.3**.

FIG. 6 shows an output converter for supplying a one-phase output current. The current supplied through the single line **1.4** is separated into two currents and one of them is inverted. The inverter **6.1** includes a transformer with oppositely connected windings and a nullifier **2.4** connected with both windings.

FIG. 7 shows an output converter for supplying a direct current. It provides separation of one of the currents into two currents and conversion of one of them by the inverter **2.3**. Both current without inverting and after the inverter **2.3** pass through diodes **7.1** connected with the same polarity. Output points of both diodes are connected and represent an output of a signal DC **7.2**.

FIG. 8 shows a two-pole output inverter for supplying a direct current. It separates the current received from the single line into two currents and inverting one of them by the inverter **2.3**. Both currents without inverting and after the inverter **2.3** pass twice through diodes **7.1** with one polarity and diodes **8.1** connected with another polarity. Output points of both diode pairs are connected and form two polar output of the signal DC **7.2** and **8.2**.

The present invention is not limited to the details shown since various modifications and structural changes are possible without departing from the spirit of the invention.

What is desired to be protected by Letters Patent is set forth in particular in the appended claims.

Claims [7]

Hide Dependent

What is claimed is:

1. A system for charging electrically driven vehicles, comprising a source of electrical current selected from the group consisting of three-phase current and one-phase current; first converting means for converting the electric current received from the

source into a converted electric current; a single electric current transmission line transmitting the converted electric current; second converting means for converting the converted electric current received through the single electric current transmission line into an electric current selected from the group consisting of three-phase electric current, one phase electric current and direct current; a plurality of charging stations connected with the second converting means for receiving from the latter at least one of the three-phase electric current, one phase electric current, and direct current, and provided with charging means for charging electrically driven vehicles with the at least one of the currents received from the second converting means.

2. The system of claim 1, wherein the single electrical current transmission line extends in ground.

3. The system of claim 1, wherein the first converting means includes a system of three transformers, with electric currents of each phase of the source of three-phase electric current supplied to each of primary windings of the transformers, with a secondary winding of one of the transformers connected opposite to its primary winding for inversion of the current, secondary windings of the transformers are connected in series, an upper end of the secondary winding of one of the transformers is an output of the converter, a lower end of the primary windings of one of the transformers and a lower end of the secondary winding the other of the transformers are connected with a nullifier.

4. The system of claim 1, wherein the second converting means include an output converter for providing a three-phase output current by separation of the current received through the single

line into three currents and conversion of their phases into phases which are conventionally used in a three-phase system, such that a first current passes through a phase shifter composed of a capacitor or inductor and a resister where resistance is a load of one of the phases, the phase shifter shifts the phase by 60 degrees, the current from the output of the phase shifter is supplied which is a load of the first phase line, the current from the single line also goes through an inverter and adds in a secondary winding of the transformer with the separated current from the single line through the transformer, the sum of the currents goes into a load of a second phase line, and the current of the third phase line is obtained after inverting of the separated current of the single line in the inverter.

5. The system of claim 1, wherein the second converting means include an output converter for supplying a one-phase output current, such that the current supplied through the single electric current transmission line is separated into two currents and one of them is inverted by an inverter which includes a transformer with oppositely connected windings and a nullifier connected with both windings.

6. The system of claim 1, wherein the second converting means include an output converter for supplying a direct current by providing separation of one of the currents into two currents and conversion of one of them by a converter, with both other current without inverting and after the inverter passing through diodes connected with the same polarity and having output points of both diodes are connected and representing an output of the converter.

7. The system of claim 1, wherein the second converting means include a two-pole output inverter for supplying a direct current, with It separating the current received from the single electric current transmission line into two currents and inverting one of them by the inverter, with both other currents without inverting and after the inverter passing twice through diodes with one polarity and diodes connected with another polarity, with output pints of both diode pairs connected and form two-polar output of the converter.

Wideband Omni-Directional Antenna

December 7, 2018

A wide band omni directional antenna, in which the radiation parameters are automatically correspond to the frequency of the emitted signal. It can be made by printing and used in small size transducers, for example in cellular telephones. The antenna radiator is formed as an electrically conductive plate, the electrically conductive plate which has a shape of a non-rectangular triangle having two lateral sides of different lengths with first ends of the lateral sides connected with one another in a point connectable to an electric signal source and other opposite second ends, and the electrically conductive plate also has a side which is opposite to the point connectable to the electric signal source and connects the opposite second ends of the lateral sides with each other thus forming a third side of the triangle of the non-rectangular triangle. The antenna can be built by using two joined triangles.

Description

Background of the Invention

The present invention generally relates to wideband antennas.

Today, the radiator in antennas, such as dipoles, monopoles, planar inverted-F antennas (PIFA), log periodic antennas, and fractal antennas, is formed as a direct or folded electrical line, for example, a wire or a printed line. The working frequencies of these antennas depend on the height or the length of their radiators. Therefore, these antennas can operate at certain frequencies only.

All existing antennas are built so as to provide a direction of the currents in the radiator for obtaining specified radiation parameters. This means that the antenna determines which currents should flow through its radiator. The number of such currents is limited. Therefore, even antennas with a wide frequency range do not work at all frequencies of this band. A log periodical antenna is further known, and it is a wideband antenna. However, the log periodical antenna is not omnidirectional, and it is very bulky.

A dipole and a monopole are known for its superb usage as a linear antenna. However, dipoles and also monopoles cannot be implemented as an internal antenna in devices that include a printed circuit board (PCB).

For example, in cellular handsets and other mobile devices, their small PCB cannot be as a ground plane for needed potential zeroing due to their small perimeter [2].

Accordingly, it is an object of the present invention to provide a wideband omni-directional antenna that eliminates the abovementioned disadvantages of the prior art antennas and has only one radiating element. The antenna of the present invention is an omni-directional wideband antenna that has a radiator formed as an electrically conductive plate.

The known wideband antennas operate using several separate radiators and thus have several resonance frequencies so that between these frequencies, the parameters of the antennas deteriorate. The wideband antenna of the present invention avoids the disadvantages of the known wideband antennas by operating with needed parameters at all frequencies of a required wide-frequency band.

In the antenna according to the present invention, the radiator is a plate in which an infinite number of currents can flow. A main part of the electric current will flow through the radiator over a distance whose length is equal to an odd number of quarters of the wavelength. As will be seen below, the resistance for such a current is minimal. Therefore, the value of this current will be maximal.

A wideband antenna according to the present invention can have a triangular form. In this case, an electric signal can be fed to a lower corner point of the triangle. The two sides of an angle at the lower corner of the triangle have different lengths. A longer side is not shorter than a quarter of the wavelength of the lowest frequency of a predetermined frequency range, while a shorter side is no longer than a quarter of the wavelength of the highest frequency of this frequency range. It is desirable that the small side is not a horizontal line.

When a signal is applied, the currents in the radiator can flow in different directions. Each direction is characterized by its resistance. According to the laws of electrical engineering, a maximum current will flow in the direction with a minimal resistance. Such minimal resistance will have a direction with a length equal to a quarter of the wavelength at a given frequency with which the antenna must operate. This resistance (R) is active and equals to an approximately active resistance of monopole with length equals to a quarter of a wavelength. If the length of a current path is different from a quarter of wavelength, then the resistance for current will be more and will be complex (Z):

where X is a reactive part of an antenna radiation resistance. Thus, for each frequency, the radiation will be created by a current flowing over a distance with a length equals to a length of a quarter of a wavelength.

Since a triangle with nonequal sides has an asymmetrical shape, its radiation can have a nonhorizontal form diagram. To obtain a radiation with a symmetrical shape in a horizontal direction, two not isosceles triangles connected by sides of the same length can be used.

The proposed antenna can have an infinitely wide band, also like a monopole has a minimum active resistance not only when its length is equal to one-quarter of a wave. The resistance of the proposed antenna will be minimal and with a length equal to an odd number of quarters of the wavelength.

According to a further novel feature of the present invention, a length of a longest one of the lateral sides is not shorter than a quarter of a wavelength of a radiation of a desired lower frequency, while a length of a shortest one of the lateral sides is no longer than a quarter of a wavelength of a radiation of a desired highest frequency.

According to a further novel feature of the present invention, the electrically conductive plate has a shape of two triangles each formed as a nonrectangular triangle of claim 1 and adjoining each other by their equal sides.

According to a further novel feature of the present invention, the two triangles are shortened at their sides opposite to the point connectable to the electrical signal source and additionally connected at their shortened sides with one another by an electrically conductive strip.

According to a further novel feature of the present invention, the electrically conductive plate can have a plurality of going through openings. Transceiver elements operating at frequencies below the radiating frequencies used can be placed in these openings.

The novel features of the present invention are set forth in detail in the appended claims. The invention itself, however, both as to its construction and its method of operation, will be best understood from the following description of the preferred embodiments, which is accompanied by the following drawings.

Brief Description of the Drawings

Figure 1 of the drawings is a view showing a triangular-form radiator of a wideband antenna according to the present invention for transmitting or receiving signals with wavelengths from λL till λH.

Figure 2 of the drawings is a view showing a double triangular-form radiator of the wideband antennas according to the present invention for transmitting or receiving signals with wavelengths from λL till λH.

Figure 3 of the drawings is a view showing a nullifier of the wideband antenna according to the present invention, formed on a basis of time delay.

Figure 4 of the drawings is a view showing a nullifier of the wideband antenna according to the present invention, in the form of a segment of a closed line.

Figure 5 of the drawings is a view showing a nullifier on a metal plate of the wideband antenna according to the present invention.

Figure 6 of the drawings is a view showing the wideband antenna according to the present invention with a double triangle radiator and a PCB in a large cellular phone.

Figure 7 of the drawings is a view showing a voltage standing wave ratio (VSWR) as a result of a simulation using the construction of the radiator shown in Figure 6 in the wideband antenna according to the present invention.

Figure 8 of the drawings is a view showing a maximal field density at a distance of 1 m and again as a result of a simulation using the construction in Figure 6 in the wideband antenna according to the present invention.

Figure 9 of the drawings is a view showing changing a maximal field density around the radiator at a distance of 1 m as a result of a simulation using the construction in Figure 6 of the wideband antenna according to the present invention.

Figure 10 of the drawings is a view showing a possible combination of a double triangle radiator and a PCB of the wideband antenna according to the present invention, in a small cellular phone.

Figure 11 of the drawings is a view showing a voltage standing wave ratio (VSWR) as a result of a simulation using the construction in Figure 10 of the wideband antenna according to the present invention.

Figure 12 of the drawings is a view showing a maximal field density at a distance of 1 m and again as a result of a simulation using the construction in Figure 10 of the wideband antenna according to the present invention.

Figure 13 of the drawings is a view showing a change of maximal field density around the radiator at a distance of 1 m as a result of a simulation using the construction in Figure 10 shown in detail of the wideband antenna according to the present invention.

Figure 14 of the drawings is a view showing an experimental model of the wideband antenna according to the present invention.

Figure 15 of the drawings is a view showing measurements of the parameter values of the antenna model of Figure 14 of the wideband antenna according to the present invention.

Figure 16 of the drawings is a view showing measurements of the directivity values of the antenna model of Figure 14 of the wideband antenna according to the present invention.

Figure 17 of the drawings is a view showing different versions (b, c, and d) of the proposed antenna by comparison with a well-known monopole (a).

Figure 18 of the drawings is a view showing holes in an antenna radiator for placing elements that do not work on a frequency of radiation of the antenna.

Description of the Preferred Embodiments

Throughout this description, the term "wideband antenna" is used to indicate a linear antenna having a single radiating element and an element for potential zeroing if it needs it. Zeroing is not needed if two same radiating elements are used like in a dipole.

Today there are many different small transducers in which it is impossible to use an antenna like a dipole. In these devices, one-side radiators like monopoles are used. In this case, the antenna is contacted with one pole of a source. Another pole of the source must have a zero potential. It is usual in these cases to utilize a ground plane, which is a printed circuit board (PCB). However, if PCB is small, zeroing of potential will not be achieved. In these cases, a nullifier has been recently utilized, as disclosed in [11]. There are different nullifiers for different transducers and for different frequencies.

There are many types of transducers that must work at several frequencies, for example, cell phones. In these cases, an antenna that has several resonance frequencies is used, for example, a planar inverted-F antenna (PIFA).

There are different wideband antennas that allow operation at many resonance frequencies. However, these antennas need tuning at non resonance frequencies [6].

The present antenna uses a radiator that resides in a flat, non flat, or flexible surface plate for various applications. This antenna has approximately the same parameters at all frequencies without any tuning. It can work within a very wideband without using grounding. Examples below correspond to cell phones operating in the frequency band 0.7–2.5 GHz.

Figure 1*a* shows a radiator of the wideband antenna according to the present invention, in the form of a triangular electrically conductive metal plate (**1.1**). The electrically conductive metal plate can be flat or can be non flat, for example, bent, etc. One port of a source of electrical signal (**1.2**) is connected with two plate sides in a point (**1.3**). Another port of the source is connected with a nullifier (**1.4**). The shortest side (**1.5**) and the longest side (**1.6**) of the radiator have lengths, correspondingly, not longer than one-quarter of the wavelength of the highest frequency and not shorter than one-quarter of the wavelength of the lowest frequency of a desirable frequency band of operation of the antenna. Figure 1*b* schematically illustrates a radiation diagram of the proposed radiator.

Figure 2*a* schematically illustrates a proposed radiator of the wideband antenna according to the present invention, in the form of a double triangle metal plate (**2.1**). The common side (**2.2**) of the triangles corresponds to one-quarter of the high-frequency wavelength. The outer sides (**2.3**) correspond to one-quarter of the low-frequency wavelength. Figure 2*b* schematically illustrates a proposed radiator formed as a different double triangle formed metallic plate (**2.1**). The common side (**2.3**) corresponds to one-quarter of the low-frequency wavelength. The outer sides (**2.2**) correspond to one-quarter of the high-frequency wavelength. In both triangles, one port of the source (**1.2**) is connected with two sides in a vertex (**1.3**). The other port of the source is connected with the nullifier (**1.4**). Figure 2*c* schematically illustrates a radiation diagram of the radiators shown in Figures 2*a* and 2*b*.

A nullifier (**3.1**) using time delay of the wideband antenna according to the present invention is shown in Figure 3. This delay is equal to half of the wave signal period or an odd number of such delays in [2]. The delay line can be made as a strip line. The nullifier used in the wideband antenna according to the present invention is disclosed, for example, in [1] for working at one frequency.

A nullifier of the wideband antenna according to the present invention using a closed line segment (**4.1**) is illustrated in Figure 4. The external side (**4.2**) of this line has a length equal to half of the wavelength at low frequency. The internal side (**4.3**) of this line has a length equal to half the wavelength at high frequency.

Figure 5 schematically illustrates a further nullifier using a metal plate or PCB (**5.1**). The sum of sides of this nullifier must be more than half wavelength.

The wideband antenna according to the present invention with a combination of the double triangle radiator (**2.1**) and PSB (**5.1**) in a "large" cellular phone is shown in Figure 6. All dimensions of the components are provided in mm.

In Figure 7 of the drawings, a voltage standing wave ratio (VSWR) of the wideband antenna according to the present invention as a result of simulation using the construction in Figure 6 is presented. The source input resistance here is equal to 100 ohms.

In Figure 8 of the drawings, a maximal field density of the wideband antenna according to the present invention at a distance of 1 m and again as a result of simulation using the construction in Figure 6 is presented. These results show that the main parameters of the wideband antenna according to the present invention practically do not depend on frequency. These parameters are close to the parameters of the tuned dipoles.

In Figure 9 of the drawings, change of maximal field density around the radiator of the wideband antenna according to the present invention at a distance of 1 m as a result of simulation using the construction on Figure bis presented. The results show that the antenna emits practically the same in all directions. The main parameters of a "large" antenna version of the wideband antenna according to the present invention at different frequencies

Figure 10 further schematically illustrates a wideband antenna according to the present invention with a combination of a double triangle radiator (**2.1**) and a PCB (**5.1**) in a "small" cellular phone. Ali dimensions are given in mm. In this case, the height of the double triangle was decreased, and an upper conductive line (**10.1**) was added. This improves a short monopole by turning it into a "T-antenna."

A view showing a VSWR in the wideband antenna according to the present invention as a result of simulation using the construction in Figure 10 is presented in Figure 11. The source input resistance here is equal to 100 ohms.

A further view illustrating a maximal field density of the wideband antenna according to the present invention at a distance of 1 m and again as a result of simulation using the construction in Figure 6 is presented in Figure 12. These results show that the main parameters of this antenna practically do not depend on frequency.

In Figure 13 of the drawings is a view showing a change of a maximal field density around the radiator at a distance of 1 m of the wideband antenna according to the present invention as a result of simulation using the construction in Figure 10. The results show that the antenna emits practically the same in all directions.

The main parameters of a "small" antenna version of the wideband antenna according to the present invention at different frequencies

An experimental model of the proposed wideband antenna according to the present invention is shown in Figure 14 (photo).

Figure 15 (photo) is a view showing the measurement values of parameter S**21** of the wideband antenna according to the present invention, which correspond to a field density at a distance of 1 m. These results confirm that in the wideband antenna according to the present invention basic parameters do not depend on frequencies within a needed frequency band.

It can be seen from the data in Figure 16 of the drawings showing the antenna model that the wideband antenna according to the present invention is omni-directional.

Various variants of the proposed antennas can be constructed as shown in Figure 17. Option **17a** is a well-known monopole, given for comparison. Option **17b** is an antenna with a rectangular radiator and with a beveled upper side. Option **17c** is an option with a triangular radiator. Option **17d** is an option with a double triangular radiator. In each version, the antenna emission bandwidth is at a level of 3 dB. It can be seen that in all embodiments according to the present invention, there is a wider band than in a monopole with a linear radiator. In cases of a small transducer, it is possible to use an electrically conductive plate with holes. In these holes, elements of a circuitry can be provided, which do not operate at a working radiating frequency. It can be seen from Figure 18 that these holes do not deteriorate the main parameters of an antenna.

All the results presented above in the figures and tables confirm that the wideband antenna according to the present invention operates almost identically at all frequencies of a wide range.

In fact, the frequency range can be significantly expanded. This follows from the fact that the radiator of the wideband antenna according to the present invention operates both with its quarter wavelength and with an odd number of quarters of the wavelength, i.e., increasing frequency. However, in this case, it is necessary to take into account the changes in the radiation resistance of the antenna. Methods for taking into account the changes in the radiation resistance of the antenna are disclosed, for example, in [6].

The present invention is not limited to the details disclosed above since various modifications and structural changes are possible without departing from the spirit of the invention.

What is desired to be protected by Letters Patent is set forth in particular in the appended claims in the present application.

Claims

1. An omni-directional wideband antenna, having a single radiator consisting exclusively of a single electrically conductive plate, wherein the single electrically conductive plate has a shape of a single nonrectangular triangle having all straight sides including

two straight lateral sides of different lengths with first ends of the lateral sides connected with one another in a point connectable to an electric signal source and other opposite second ends; wherein the single electrically conductive plate also has a straight side that is opposite to the point connectable to the electric signal source and connects the opposite second ends of the lateral sides with each other, thus forming a third side of the nonrectangular triangle; and wherein a length of a longest one of the lateral sides is not shorter than a quarter of a wavelength of a radiation of a desired lower frequency, while a length of a shortest one of the lateral sides is no longer than a quarter of a wavelength of a radiation of a desired highest frequency.

2. The antenna of claim 1, wherein the single electrically conductive plate has a plurality of going through openings.

Patent History

Patent number: 10381744
Type: Grant
Filed: December 7, 2018
Date of Patent: Aug 13, 2019
Inventor: Michael Bank (Jerusalem)
Primary Examiner: Ricardo I. Magallanes
Application Number: 16/213,738

Classifications

Current US Class: Including Balanced Doublet-type Antenna (343/727)
International Classification: H01Q 21/20 (20060101), H01Q 3/42

(20060101), H01Q 3/22 (20060101), H01Q 5/15 (20150101), H01Q 9/30 (20060101)

US *Patent* No. 10305289.Phase converter for vector conversion of three-phase signals

- <u>System and Method for Translocation and Buffering Cellular Radiation Source</u>

Publication number: 20220302575

10381744

US *Patent* No. 10305289.Phase converter for vector conversion of three-phase signals

- 9246405B2
- US10250061B1
- *Electrical energy transmission system which does not require reservation*

Patent number: 11258268P34

Abstract: An electric energy transmission system which does not need a reservation has a generator generating a multi-phase electric current, a converter converting it into another electric current, an electric current network connected with the converter and having a first group of electric current lines extending towards electric current users and a second group of electric current ones electrically connecting the electric current lines of the first group with each other, and a plurality of consumer blocks connected with the network and having users which use different electric currents and further converters converting the electric current transmitted by the network into the different electric currents and supplying the different electric currents to the electric current users.

Type: Grant
Filed: May 11, 2021
Date of Patent: February 22, 2022
Inventor: Michael Bank
US6297971B1P 28

10250061P29

9,608,441 **P8** and 9,246,405 **P9**

One-wire method main patent
US Patent 9608441B

Single-wire electric transmission line

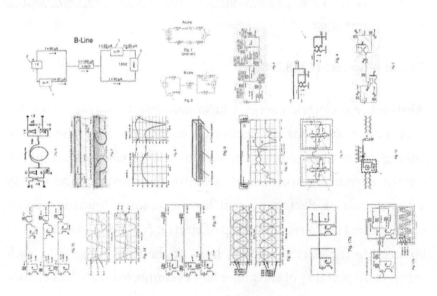

Classifications

<u>H02J3/00</u> Circuit arrangements for ac mains or ac distribution networks

V One-wire method main patent
US Patent 9608441B2P2

- *SYSTEM AND METHOD FOR TRANSLOCATING AND BUFFERING CELLULAR RADIATION SOURCE*

Publication number: 20220302575

Abstract: System and method for reduction of exposure to electromagnetic radiation emitted while using a communication network, wherein said electromagnetic radiation can potentially cause vulnerabilities to the human body or to the data integrity conveyed thereby by the translocating and buffering of a transceiver electromagnetic radiation signal by using an intermediary relay system or method.

Type: Application
Filed: September 7, 2020
Publication date: September 22, 2022
Inventors: Michael BANK, Carmi HALACHMI, Eugene SHUBOV

- *Electrical energy transmission system which does not require reservation*

Patent number: 11258268

Abstract: An electric energy transmission system which does not need a reservation has a generator generating a multi-phase electric current, a converter converting it into another electric current, an electric current network connected with the converter and having a first group of electric current lines extending towards electric current users and a second group of electric current ones electrically connecting the electric current lines of the first group with each other, and a plurality of consumer blocks connected with the network and having users which use different electric currents and further converters converting the electric current transmitted by the network into the different electric currents and supplying the different electric currents to the electric current users.

Type: Grant
Filed: May 11, 2021
Date of Patent: February 22, 2022
Inventor: Michael Bank

- *Setting overrides*

Patent number: 11258746

Abstract: Techniques for managing notifications to be presented by user devices are described. In an example, a computer system associates a first user account with a user device and stores first data indicating that a notification about a communications session via a communications network system is prohibited. The computer system receives a request associated with the first user account for com

- *Wide band omni directional antenna*

Patent number: 10381744

Abstract: A wide band omni directional antenna, in which the radiation parameters are automatically correspond to the frequency of the emitted signal. It can be made by printing and used in small size transducers, for example in cellular telephones. The antenna radiator is formed as an electrically conductive plate, the electrically conductive plate which has a shape of a non-rectangular triangle having two lateral sides of different lengths with first ends of the lateral sides connected with one another in a point connectable to an electric signal source and other opposite second ends, and the electrically conductive plate also has a side which is opposite to the point connectable to the electric signal source and connects the opposite second ends of the lateral sides with each other thus forming a third side of the triangle of the non-rectangular triangle. The antenna can be built by using two joined triangles.

Type: Grant
Filed: December 7, 2018
Date of Patent: August 13, 2019
Inventor: Michael Bank

- *Phase converter for vector conversion of three phase signals*

Patent number: 10305289

Abstract: A phase converter for electrical signals is configured for obtaining a vector sum of phase signals or subdividing one signal into several phase signals, including transformers and configured for successive addition of signals received from secondary windings of

the transformers and inversion of one or several of the signals, or for subdivision of the one signal into the several phase signals.

Type: Grant
Filed: November 20, 2017
Date of Patent: May 28, 2019
Inventor: Michael Bank

- *PHASE CONVERTER FOR VECTOR CONVERSION OF THREE PHASE SIGNALS*

Publication number: 20190157875

Abstract: A phase converter for electrical signals is configured for obtaining a vector sum of phase signals or subdividing one signal into several phase signals, including transformers and configured for successive addition of signals received from secondary windings of the transformers and inversion of one or several of the signals, or for subdivision of the one signal into the several phase signals.

Type: Application
Filed: November 20, 2017
Publication date: May 23, 2019
Inventor: Michael Bank

- *System for charging electrically drive vehicles with a single line for transmitting electric current from a source to a charging station*

Patent number: 10250061

Abstract: A system for charging electrically driven vehicles includes a source of three phase electrical current, a first converter converting the three-phase or one-phase electric current received from the source into a converted electric current, a single electric current transmission line transmitting the converted electric current, a second converter converting the converted signal received through the single line into three phase electric current, or one phase electric current, or direct current, and a plurality of charging stations receiving from the second converter corresponding currents and provided with charging components for charging electrically driven vehicles with a corresponding one of the received currents.

Type: Grant
Filed: May 8, 2018
Date of Patent: April 2, 2019
Inventor: Michael Bank
Inventor: Michael Bank

- *Wide band antenna*

Patent number: 10050353

Abstract: A wide band antenna has a first radiator formed as an electrical field signal monopole radiator or a helix radiator, and a second radiator formed as an electric field folded dipole radiator or as a magnetic field loop radiator, with the first radiator radiating a signal at a lowest frequency and its odd harmonics and the second radiator radiating a signal at even harmonics of the lowest frequency.

Type: Grant
Filed: December 30, 2016
Date of Patent: August 14, 2018
Inventors: Michael Bank, Motti Haridim

- *WIDE BAND ANTENNA*

Publication number: 20180191084

Abstract: A wide band antenna has a first radiator formed as an electrical field signal monopole radiator or a helix radiator, and a second radiator formed as an electric field folded dipole radiator or as a magnetic field loop radiator, with the first radiator radiating a signal at a lowest frequency and its odd harmonics and the second radiator radiating a signal at even harmonics of the lowest frequency.

Type: Application
Filed: December 30, 2016
Publication date: July 5, 2018
Inventors: MICHAEL BANK, Motti Haridim
Inventor: Michael Bank

- *Surface antenna with a single radiation element*

Patent number: 9685704

Abstract: A surface antenna with a single radiation element, which comprises (a) a power source with first and second poles; (b) a phase shifting element, inserted to the path of one of the poles of the power source in such a manner that the phase shifting device shifts the phase of a first signal propagating through said pole such that the shifted phase of the first signal will be essentially identical to the phase of a second signal propagating through the other pole. The shifted first signal is added to the second signal with essentially the same phase of second signal, whenever both poles are connected together to form a single-wire, through which the resulting added signal propagates.

Type: Grant
Filed: January 17, 2013
Date of Patent: June 20, 2017
Inventors: Michael Bank, Motti Haridim

- Single-wire electric transmission line

Patent number: 9608441

Abstract: A single-wire electric transmission line system that includes a power sources having first and second poles and a phase shifting device, coupled to one of the poles of the power source, in such a manner that the phase shifting device shifts the phase of a first signal propagating through the pole such that the shifted phase of the first signal will be essentially identical to the phase of a second signal propagating through the other pole. The shifted first signal is added to the second signal with essentially the same phase of second signal, whenever both poles are connected together to form a single-wire, through which the resulting added signal propagates.

Type: Grant
Filed: February 4, 2014
Date of Patent: March 28, 2017
Assignee: SLE INTERNATIONAL LLC.
Inventor: Michael Bank

- *Electrical energy transmission system with a single transmission line*

Patent number: 9246405

Abstract: An electrical energy transmission system has a three-phase electric current power source which generates a three-phase electric current having three electric currents, a converting device which converts the three-phase electric current to obtain a common electric current signal formed by summation of three electric currents having the same phases, and a single-line electrical transmission line which transmits further the thusly produced common electric current signal.

Type: Grant
Filed: November 28, 2014
Date of Patent: January 26, 2016
Assignee: SLE INTERNATIONAL, LLC
Inventor: Michael Bank

- *ELECTRICAL ENERGY TRANSMISSION SYSTEM*

Publication number: 20150229232

Abstract: An electrical energy transmission system has a three-phase electric current power source which generates a three-phase electric current having three electric currents, a converting device which converts the three-phase electric current to obtain a common electric current signal formed by summation of three electric currents having the same phases, and a single-line electrical transmission line which transmits further the thusly produced common electric current signal.

Type: Application

Filed: November 28, 2014

Publication date: August 13, 2015

Inventor: Michael Bank

- *Apparatus for reducing vibrations in a vehicle*
- *SYSTEM AND METHOD FOR TRANSLOCATING AND BUFFERING CELLULAR RADIATION SOURCE*

Publication number: 20220302575

Abstract: System and method for reduction of exposure to electromagnetic radiation emitted while using a communication network, wherein said electromagnetic radiation can potentially cause vulnerabilities to the human body or to the data integrity conveyed thereby by the translocating and buffering of a transceiver electromagnetic radiation signal by using an intermediary relay system or method.

Type: Application

Filed: September 7, 2020

Publication date: September 22, 2022

Inventors: Michael BANK, Carmi HALACHMI, Eugene SHUBOV

- *trical energy transmission system which does not require reservation*

Patent number: 11258268

Abstract: An electric energy transmission system which does not need a reservation has a generator generating a multi-phase electric current, a converter converting it into another electric current, an electric current network connected with the converter and having a first group of electric current lines extending towards electric current users and a second group of electric current ones electrically connecting the electric current lines of the first group with each other, and a plurality of consumer blocks connected with the network and having users which use different electric currents and further converters converting the electric current transmitted by the network into the different electric currents and supplying the different electric currents to the electric current users.

Type: Grant
Filed: May 11, 2021
Date of Patent: February 22, 2022
Inventor: Michael Bank

- *Setting overrides*

Patent number: 11258746

Abstract: Techniques for managing notifications to be presented by user devices are described. In an example, a computer system associates a first user account with a user device and stores first data indicating that a notification about a communications session via a communications network system is prohibited. The computer system receives a request associated with the first user account for communications with another device via the communications network system. Based at least in part on the other device, the computer system generates second data indicating that the notification about the communications session is to be presented within a period of time of the communications session being requested. The computer system associates the first user account with the second data.

Type: Grant

Filed: April 18, 2019

Date of Patent: February 22, 2022

Assignee: Amazon Technologies, Inc.

Inventors: Vinaya Nadig, Sarang Anil Ozarde, Shawn Michael Banks, King Lung Chiu, Nicholas Kalkouni, Brian Oliver, Anuj Kamra, Iain Kennedy, Tu Dien Do, Adri

- *Wide band omni directional antenna*

Patent number: 10381744

Abstract: A wide band omni directional antenna, in which the radiation parameters are automatically correspond to the frequency of the emitted signal. It can be made by printing and used in small size transducers, for example in cellular telephones. The antenna radiator is formed as an electrically conductive plate, the electrically conductive plate which has a shape of a non-rectangular triangle having two lateral sides of different lengths with first ends of the lateral sides connected with one another in a point connectable to an electric signal source and other opposite second ends, and the electrically conductive plate also has a side which is opposite to the point connectable to the electric signal source and connects the opposite second ends of the lateral sides with each other thus forming a third side of the triangle of the non-rectangular triangle. The antenna can be built by using two joined triangles.

Type: Grant

Filed: December 7, 2018

Date of Patent: August 13, 2019

Inventor: Michael Bank

- *Phase converter for vector conversion of three phase signals*

Patent number: 10305289

Abstract: A phase converter for electrical signals is configured for obtaining a vector sum of phase signals or subdividing one signal into several phase signals, including transformers and configured for successive addition of signals received from secondary windings of the transformers and inversion of one or several of the signals, or for subdivision of the one signal into the several phase signals.

Type: Grant
Filed: November 20, 2017
Date of Patent: May 28, 2019
Inventor: Michael Bank

- *PHASE CONVERTER FOR VECTOR CONVERSION OF THREE PHASE SIGNALS*

Publication number: 20190157875

Abstract: A phase converter for electrical signals is configured for obtaining a vector sum of phase signals or subdividing one signal into several phase signals, including transformers and configured for successive addition of signals received from secondary windings of the transformers and inversion of one or several of the signals, or for subdivision of the one signal into the several phase signals.

Type: Application
Filed: November 20, 2017
Publication date: May 23, 2019
Inventor: Michael Bank

- *System for charging electrically drive vehicles with a single line for transmitting electric current from a source to a charging station*

Patent number: 10250061

Abstract: A system for charging electrically driven vehicles includes a source of three phase electrical current, a first converter converting the three-phase or one-phase electric current received from the source into a converted electric current, a single electric current transmission line transmitting the converted electric current, a second converter converting the converted signal received through the single line into three phase electric current, or one phase electric current, or direct current, and a plurality of charging stations receiving from the second converter corresponding currents and provided with charging components for charging electrically driven vehicles with a corresponding one of the received currents.

Type: Grant
Filed: May 8, 2018
Date of Patent: April 2, 2019
Inventor: Michael Bank

- *Wide band omni directional antenna*

Patent number: 10381744

Abstract: A wide band omni directional antenna, in which the radiation parameters are automatically correspond to the frequency of the emitted signal. It can be made by printing and used in small size transducers, for example in cellular telephones. The antenna radiator is formed as an electrically conductive plate, the electrically

conductive plate which has a shape of a non-rectangular triangle having two lateral sides of different lengths with first ends of the lateral sides connected with one another in a point connectable to an electric signal source and other opposite second ends, and the electrically conductive plate also has a side which is opposite to the point connectable to the electric signal source and connects the opposite second ends of the lateral sides with each other thus forming a third side of the triangle of the non-rectangular triangle. The antenna can be built by using two joined triangles.

Type: Grant
Filed: December 7, 2018
Date of Patent: August 13, 2019
Inventor: Michael Bank

- *Phase converter for vector conversion of three phase signals*

Patent number: 10305289

Abstract: A phase converter for electrical signals is configured for obtaining a vector sum of phase signals or subdividing one signal into several phase signals, including transformers and configured for successive addition of signals received from secondary windings of the transformers and inversion of one or several of the signals, or for subdivision of the one signal into the several phase signals.

Type: Grant
Filed: November 20, 2017
Date of Patent: May 28, 2019
Inventor: Michael Bank

- *PHASE CONVERTER FOR VECTOR CONVERSION OF THREE PHASE SIGNALS*

Publication number: 20190157875

Abstract: A phase converter for electrical signals is configured for obtaining a vector sum of phase signals or subdividing one signal into several phase signals, including transformers and configured for successive addition of signals received from secondary windings of the transformers and inversion of one or several of the signals, or for subdivision of the one signal into the several phase signals.

Type: Application
Filed: November 20, 2017
Publication date: May 23, 2019
Inventor: Michael Bank

- *System for charging electrically drive vehicles with a single line for transmitting electric current from a source to a charging station*

Patent number: 10250061

Abstract: A system for charging electrically driven vehicles includes a source of three phase electrical current, a first converter converting the three-phase or one-phase electric current received from the source into a converted electric current, a single electric current transmission line transmitting the converted electric current, a second converter converting the converted signal received through the single line into three phase electric current, or one phase electric current, or direct current, and a plurality of charging stations receiving from the second converter corresponding currents and provided with

charging components for charging electrically driven vehicles with a corresponding one of the received currents.

Type: Grant
Filed: May 8, 2018
Date of Patent: April 2, 2019
Inventor: Michael Bank

- *Wide band omni directional antenna*

Patent number: 10381744

Abstract: A wide band omni directional antenna, in which the radiation parameters are automatically correspond to the frequency of the emitted signal. It can be made by printing and used in small size transducers, for example in cellular telephones. The antenna radiator is formed as an electrically conductive plate, the electrically conductive plate which has a shape of a non-rectangular triangle having two lateral sides of different lengths with first ends of the lateral sides connected with one another in a point connectable to an electric signal source and other opposite second ends, and the electrically conductive plate also has a side which is opposite to the point connectable to the electric signal source and connects the opposite second ends of the lateral sides with each other thus forming a third side of the triangle of the non-rectangular triangle. The antenna can be built by using two joined triangles.

Type: Grant
Filed: December 7, 2018
Date of Patent: August 13, 2019
Inventor: Michael Bank

- *Phase converter for vector conversion of three phase signals*

Patent number: 10305289

Abstract: A phase converter for electrical signals is configured for obtaining a vector sum of phase signals or subdividing one signal into several phase signals, including transformers and configured for successive addition of signals received from secondary windings of the transformers and inversion of one or several of the signals, or for subdivision of the one signal into the several phase signals.

Type: Grant
Filed: November 20, 2017
Date of Patent: May 28, 2019
Inventor: Michael Bank

- *PHASE CONVERTER FOR VECTOR CONVERSION OF THREE PHASE SIGNALS*

Publication number: 20190157875

Abstract: A phase converter for electrical signals is configured for obtaining a vector sum of phase signals or subdividing one signal into several phase signals, including transformers and configured for successive addition of signals received from secondary windings of the transformers and inversion of one or several of the signals, or for subdivision of the one signal into the several phase signals.

Type: Application
Filed: November 20, 2017
Publication date: May 23, 2019
Inventor: Michael Bank

- *System for charging electrically drive vehicles with a single line for transmitting electric current from a source to a charging station*

Patent number: 10250061

Abstract: A system for charging electrically driven vehicles includes a source of three phase electrical current, a first converter converting the three-phase or one-phase electric current received from the source into a converted electric current, a single electric current transmission line transmitting the converted electric current, a second converter converting the converted signal received through the single line into three phase electric current, or one phase electric current, or direct current, and a plurality of charging stations receiving from the second converter corresponding currents and provided with charging components for charging electrically driven vehicles with a corresponding one of the received currents.

Type: Grant
Filed: May 8, 2018
Date of Patent: April 2, 2019
Inventor: Michael Bank

- *Wide band omni directional antenna*

Patent number: 10381744

Abstract: A wide band omni directional antenna, in which the radiation parameters are automatically correspond to the frequency of the emitted signal. It can be made by printing and used in small size transducers, for example in cellular telephones. The antenna radiator is formed as an electrically conductive plate, the electrically

conductive plate which has a shape of a non-rectangular triangle having two lateral sides of different lengths with first ends of the lateral sides connected with one another in a point connectable to an electric signal source and other opposite second ends, and the electrically conductive plate also has a side which is opposite to the point connectable to the electric signal source and connects the opposite second ends of the lateral sides with each other thus forming a third side of the triangle of the non-rectangular triangle. The antenna can be built by using two joined triangles.

Type: Grant
Filed: December 7, 2018
Date of Patent: August 13, 2019
Inventor: Michael Bank

- *Phase converter for vector conversion of three phase signals*

Patent number: 10305289

Abstract: A phase converter for electrical signals is configured for obtaining a vector sum of phase signals or subdividing one signal into several phase signals, including transformers and configured for successive addition of signals received from secondary windings of the transformers and inversion of one or several of the signals, or for subdivision of the one signal into the several phase signals.

Type: Grant
Filed: November 20, 2017
Date of Patent: May 28, 2019
Inventor: Michael Bank

- *PHASE CONVERTER FOR VECTOR CONVERSION OF THREE PHASE SIGNALS*

Publication number: 20190157875

Abstract: A phase converter for electrical signals is configured for obtaining a vector sum of phase signals or subdividing one signal into several phase signals, including transformers and configured for successive addition of signals received from secondary windings of the transformers and inversion of one or several of the signals, or for subdivision of the one signal into the several phase signals.

Type: Application
Filed: November 20, 2017
Publication date: May 23, 2019
Inventor: Michael Bank

- *System for charging electrically drive vehicles with a single line for transmitting electric current from a source to a charging station*

Patent number: 10250061

Abstract: A system for charging electrically driven vehicles includes a source of three phase electrical current, a first converter converting the three-phase or one-phase electric current received from the source into a converted electric current, a single electric current transmission line transmitting the converted electric current, a second converter converting the converted signal received through the single line into three phase electric current, or one phase electric current, or direct current, and a plurality of charging stations receiving from the second converter corresponding currents and provided with

charging components for charging electrically driven vehicles with a corresponding one of the received currents.

Type: Grant
Filed: May 8, 2018
Date of Patent: April 2, 2019
Inventor: Michael Bank

1   Wide band omni directional antenna

Patent number: 10381744

Abstract: A wide band omni directional antenna, in which the radiation parameters are automatically correspond to the frequency of the emitted signal. It can be made by printing and used in small size transducers, for example in cellular telephones. The antenna radiator is formed as an electrically conductive plate, the electrically conductive plate which has a shape of a non-rectangular triangle having two lateral sides of different lengths with first ends of the lateral sides connected with one another in a point connectable to an electric signal source and other opposite second ends, and the electrically conductive plate also has a side which is opposite to the point connectable to the electric signal source and connects the opposite second ends of the lateral sides with each other thus forming a third side of the triangle of the non-rectangular triangle. The antenna can be built by using two joined triangles.

Type: Grant
Filed: December 7, 2018
Date of Patent: August 13, 2019
Inventor: Michael Bank

2   *Phase converter for vector conversion of three phase signals*

Patent number: 10305289

Abstract: A phase converter for electrical signals is configured for obtaining a vector sum of phase signals or subdividing one signal into several phase signals, including transformers and configured for successive addition of signals received from secondary windings of the transformers and inversion of one or several of the signals, or for subdivision of the one signal into the several phase signals.

Type: Grant
Filed: November 20, 2017
Date of Patent: May 28, 2019
Inventor: Michael Bank

3   *PHASE CONVERTER FOR VECTOR CONVERSION OF THREE PHASE SIGNALS*

Publication number: 20190157875

Abstract: A phase converter for electrical signals is configured for obtaining a vector sum of phase signals or subdividing one signal into several phase signals, including transformers and configured for successive addition of signals received from secondary windings of the transformers and inversion of one or several of the signals, or for subdivision of the one signal into the several phase signals.

Type: Application
Filed: November 20, 2017
Publication date: May 23, 2019
Inventor: Michael Bank

4   System for charging electrically drive vehicles with a single line for transmitting electric current from a source to a charging station

Patent number: 10250061

Abstract: A system for charging electrically driven vehicles includes a source of three phase electrical current, a first converter converting the three-phase or one-phase electric current received from the source into a converted electric current, a single electric current transmission line transmitting the converted electric current, a second converter converting the converted signal received through the single line into three phase electric current, or one phase electric current, or direct current, and a plurality of charging stations receiving from the second converter corresponding currents and provided with charging components for charging electrically driven vehicles with a corresponding one of the received currents.

Type: Grant
Filed: May 8, 2018
Date of Patent: April 2, 2019
Inventor: Michael Bank

8.Some of patents

- *SYSTEM AND METHOD FOR TRANSLOCATING AND BUFFERING CELLULAR RADIATION SOURCE*

Publication number: 20220302575

Abstract: System and method for reduction of exposure to electromagnetic radiation emitted while using a communication network, wherein said electromagnetic radiation can potentially cause vulnerabilities to the human body or to the data integrity conveyed thereby by the translocating and buffering of a transceiver electromagnetic radiation signal by using an intermediary relay system or method.

Type: Application
Filed: September 7, 2020
Publication date: September 22, 2022
Inventors: Michael BANK, Carmi HALACHMI, Eugene SHUBOV

- *Electrical energy transmission system which does not require reservation*

Patent number: 11258268

Abstract: An electric energy transmission system which does not need a reservation has a generator generating a multi-phase electric current, a converter converting it into another electric current, an electric current network connected with the converter and having a first group of electric current lines extending towards electric current users and a second group of electric current ones electrically connecting the electric current lines of the first group with each other, and a plurality of consumer blocks connected with the network and having users which use different electric currents and further converters converting the electric current transmitted by the network into the different electric currents and supplying the different electric currents to the electric current users.

Type: Grant
Filed: May 11, 2021

Date of Patent: February 22, 2022
Inventor: Michael Bank

- *Setting overrides*

Patent number: 11258746

Abstract: Techniques for managing notifications to be presented by user devices are described. In an example, a computer system associates a first user account with a user device and stores first data indicating that a notification about a communications session via a communications network system is prohibited. The computer system receives a request associated with the first user account for com

- *Wide band omni directional antenna*

Patent number: 10381744

Abstract: A wide band omni directional antenna, in which the radiation parameters are automatically correspond to the frequency of the emitted signal. It can be made by printing and used in small size transducers, for example in cellular telephones. The antenna radiator is formed as an electrically conductive plate, the electrically conductive plate which has a shape of a non-rectangular triangle having two lateral sides of different lengths with first ends of the lateral sides connected with one another in a point connectable to an electric signal source and other opposite second ends, and the electrically conductive plate also has a side which is opposite to the point connectable to the electric signal source and connects the opposite second ends of the lateral sides with each other thus forming a third side of the triangle of the non-rectangular triangle. The antenna can be built by using two joined triangles.

Type: Grant
Filed: December 7, 2018
Date of Patent: August 13, 2019
Inventor: Michael Bank

- *Phase converter for vector conversion of three phase signals*

Patent number: 10305289

Abstract: A phase converter for electrical signals is configured for obtaining a vector sum of phase signals or subdividing one signal into several phase signals, including transformers and configured for successive addition of signals received from secondary windings of the transformers and inversion of one or several of the signals, or for subdivision of the one signal into the several phase signals.

Type: Grant
Filed: November 20, 2017
Date of Patent: May 28, 2019
Inventor: Michael Bank

- *PHASE CONVERTER FOR VECTOR CONVERSION OF THREE PHASE SIGNALS*

Publication number: 20190157875

Abstract: A phase converter for electrical signals is configured for obtaining a vector sum of phase signals or subdividing one signal into several phase signals, including transformers and configured for successive addition of signals received from secondary windings of the transformers and inversion of one or several of the signals, or for subdivision of the one signal into the several phase signals.

Type: Application
Filed: November 20, 2017
Publication date: May 23, 2019
Inventor: Michael Bank

- *System for charging electrically drive vehicles with a single line for transmitting electric current from a source to a charging station*

Patent number: 10250061

Abstract: A system for charging electrically driven vehicles includes a source of three phase electrical current, a first converter converting the three-phase or one-phase electric current received from the source into a converted electric current, a single electric current transmission line transmitting the converted electric current, a second converter converting the converted signal received through the single line into three phase electric current, or one phase electric current, or direct current, and a plurality of charging stations receiving from the second converter corresponding currents and provided with charging components for charging electrically driven vehicles with a corresponding one of the received currents.

Type: Grant
Filed: May 8, 2018
Date of Patent: April 2, 2019
Inventor: Michael Bank
Inventor: Michael Bank

- *Wide band antenna*

Patent number: 10050353

Abstract: A wide band antenna has a first radiator formed as an electrical field signal monopole radiator or a helix radiator, and a second radiator formed as an electric field folded dipole radiator or as a magnetic field loop radiator, with the first radiator radiating a signal at a lowest frequency and its odd harmonics and the second radiator radiating a signal at even harmonics of the lowest frequency.

Type: Grant
Filed: December 30, 2016
Date of Patent: August 14, 2018
Inventors: Michael Bank, Motti Haridim

- *WIDE BAND ANTENNA*

Publication number: 20180191084

Abstract: A wide band antenna has a first radiator formed as an electrical field signal monopole radiator or a helix radiator, and a second radiator formed as an electric field folded dipole radiator or as a magnetic field loop radiator, with the first radiator radiating a signal at a lowest frequency and its odd harmonics and the second radiator radiating a signal at even harmonics of the lowest frequency.

Type: Application
Filed: December 30, 2016
Publication date: July 5, 2018
Inventors: MICHAEL BANK, Motti Haridim
Inventor: Michael Bank

- *Surface antenna with a single radiation element*

Patent number: 9685704

Abstract: A surface antenna with a single radiation element, which comprises (a) a power source with first and second poles; (b) a phase shifting element, inserted to the path of one of the poles of the power source in such a manner that the phase shifting device shifts the phase of a first signal propagating through said pole such that the shifted phase of the first signal will be essentially identical to the phase of a second signal propagating through the other pole. The shifted first signal is added to the second signal with essentially the same phase of second signal, whenever both poles are connected together to form a single-wire, through which the resulting added signal propagates.

Type: Grant
Filed: January 17, 2013
Date of Patent: June 20, 2017
Inventors: Michael Bank, Motti Haridim
Assignee: SLE INTERNATIONAL LLC.
Inventor: Michael Bank

Patent number: 9246405

Abstract: An electrical energy transmission system has a three-phase electric current power source which generates a three-phase electric current having three electric currents, a converting device which converts the three-phase electric current to obtain a common electric current signal formed by summation of three electric currents having the same phases, and a single-line electrical transmission line which transmits further the thusly produced common electric current signal.

Type: Grant
Filed: November 28, 2014
Date of Patent: January 26, 2016
Assignee: SLE INTERNATIONAL, LLC
Inventor: Michael Bank

ELECTRICAL ENERGY TRANSMISSION SYSTEM

Publication number: 20150229232

Abstract: An electrical energy transmission system has a three-phase electric current power source which generates a three-phase electric current having three electric currents, a converting device which converts the three-phase electric current to obtain a common electric current signal formed by summation of three electric currents having the same phases, and a single-line electrical transmission line which transmits further the thusly produced common electric current signal.

Type: Application
Filed: November 28, 2014
Publication date: August 13, 2015
Inventor: Michael Bank

Apparatus for reducing vibrations in a vehicle

SYSTEM AND METHOD FOR TRANSLOCATING AND BUFFERING CELLULAR RADIATION SOURCE

Publication number: 20220302575

Abstract: System and method for reduction of exposure to electromagnetic radiation emitted while using a communication network, wherein said electromagnetic radiation can potentially cause vulnerabilities to the human body or to the data integrity conveyed thereby by the translocating and buffering of a transceiver electromagnetic radiation signal by using an intermediary relay system or method.

Type: Application
Filed: September 7, 2020
Publication date: September 22, 2022
Inventors: Michael BANK, Carmi HALACHMI, Eugene SHUBOV

- *Tipical energy transmission system which does not require reservation*

Patent number: 11258268

Abstract: An electric energy transmission system which does not need a reservation has a generator generating a multi-phase electric current, a converter converting it into another electric current, an electric current network connected with the converter and having a first group of electric current lines extending towards electric current users and a second group of electric current ones electrically connecting the electric current lines of the first group with each other, and a plurality of consumer blocks connected with the network and having users which use different electric currents and further converters converting the electric current transmitted by the network into the different electric currents and supplying the different electric currents to the electric current users.

Type: Grant
Filed: May 11, 2021
Date of Patent: February 22, 2022
Inventor: Michael Bank

- *Setting overrides*

Patent number: 11258746

Abstract: Techniques for managing notifications to be presented by user devices are described. In an example, a computer system associates a first user account with a user device and stores first data indicating that a notification about a communications session via a communications network system is prohibited. The computer system receives a request associated with the first user account for communications with another device via the communications network system. Based at least in part on the other device, the computer system generates second data indicating that the notification about the communications session is to be presented within a period of time of the communications session being requested. The computer system associates the first user account with the second data.

Type: Grant
Filed: April 18, 2019
Date of Patent: February 22, 2022
Assignee: Amazon Technologies, Inc.

Inventors: Vinaya Nadig, Sarang Anil Ozarde, Shawn Michael Banks, King Lung Chiu, Nicholas Kalkouni, Brian Oliver, Anuj Kamra, Iain Kennedy, Tu Dien Do, Adri

Wide band omni directional antenna

Patent number: 10381744

Abstract: A wide band omni directional antenna, in which the radiation parameters are automatically correspond to the frequency of the emitted signal. It can be made by printing and used in small size transducers, for example in cellular telephones. The antenna radiator is formed as an electrically conductive plate, the electrically conductive plate which has a shape of a non-rectangular triangle having two lateral sides of different lengths with first ends of the lateral sides connected with one another in a point connectable to an electric signal source and other opposite second ends, and the electrically conductive plate also has a side which is opposite to the point connectable to the electric signal source and connects the opposite second ends of the lateral sides with each other thus forming a third side of the triangle of the non-rectangular triangle. The antenna can be built by using two joined triangles.

Type: Grant
Filed: December 7, 2018
Date of Patent: August 13, 2019
Inventor: Michael Bank

- *Phase converter for vector conversion of three phase signals*

Patent number: 10305289

Abstract: A phase converter for electrical signals is configured for obtaining a vector sum of phase signals or subdividing one signal into several phase signals, including transformers and configured for successive addition of signals received from secondary windings of

the transformers and inversion of one or several of the signals, or for subdivision of the one signal into the several phase signals.

Type: Grant
Filed: November 20, 2017
Date of Patent: May 28, 2019
Inventor: Michael Bank

PHASE CONVERTER FOR VECTOR CONVERSION OF THREE PHASE SIGNALS

Publication number: 20190157875

Abstract: A phase converter for electrical signals is configured for obtaining a vector sum of phase signals or subdividing one signal into several phase signals, including transformers and configured for successive addition of signals received from secondary windings of the transformers and inversion of one or several of the signals, or for subdivision of the one signal into the several phase signals.

Type: Application
Filed: November 20, 2017
Publication date: May 23, 2019
Inventor: Michael Bank

System for charging electrically drive vehicles with a single line for transmitting electric current from a source to a charging station

Patent number: 10250061

Abstract: A system for charging electrically driven vehicles includes a source of three phase electrical current, a first converter converting the three-phase or one-phase electric current received from the source into a converted electric current, a single electric current transmission line transmitting the converted electric current, a second converter converting the converted signal received through the single line into three phase electric current, or one phase electric current, or direct current, and a plurality of charging stations receiving from the second converter corresponding currents and provided with charging components for charging electrically driven vehicles with a corresponding one of the received currents.

Type: Grant
Filed: May 8, 2018
Date of Patent: April 2, 2019
Inventor: Michael Bank

Wide band omni directional antenna

Patent number: 10381744

Abstract: A wide band omni directional antenna, in which the radiation parameters are automatically correspond to the frequency of the emitted signal. It can be made by printing and used in small size transducers, for example in cellular telephones. The antenna radiator is formed as an electrically conductive plate, the electrically conductive plate which has a shape of a non-rectangular triangle having two lateral sides of different lengths with first ends of the lateral sides connected with one another in a point connectable to an electric signal source and other opposite second ends, and the electrically conductive plate also has a side which is opposite to the point connectable to the electric signal source and connects the opposite second ends of the lateral sides with each other thus forming a third side of the triangle of the non-rectangular triangle. The antenna can be built by using two joined triangles.

Type: Grant
Filed: December 7, 2018
Date of Patent: August 13, 2019
Inventor: Michael Bank

Phase converter for vector conversion of three phase signals

Patent number: 10305289

Abstract: A phase converter for electrical signals is configured for obtaining a vector sum of phase signals or subdividing one signal into several phase signals, including transformers and configured for successive addition of signals received from secondary windings of the transformers and inversion of one or several of the signals, or for subdivision of the one signal into the several phase signals.

Type: Grant
Filed: November 20, 2017
Date of Patent: May 28, 2019
Inventor: Michael Bank

PHASE CONVERTER FOR VECTOR CONVERSION OF THREE PHASE SIGNALS

Publication number: 20190157875

Abstract: A phase converter for electrical signals is configured for obtaining a vector sum of phase signals or subdividing one signal into several phase signals, including transformers and configured for successive addition of signals received from secondary windings of the transformers and inversion of one or several of the signals, or for subdivision of the one signal into the several phase signals.

Type: Application
Filed: November 20, 2017
Publication date: May 23, 2019
Inventor: Michael Bank

System for charging electrically drive vehicles with a single line for transmitting electric current from a source to a charging station

Patent number: 10250061

Abstract: A system for charging electrically driven vehicles includes a source of three phase electrical current, a first converter converting the three-phase or one-phase electric current received from the source into a converted electric current, a single electric current transmission line transmitting the converted electric current, a second converter converting the converted signal received through the single line into three phase electric current, or one phase electric current, or direct current, and a plurality of charging stations receiving from the second converter corresponding currents and provided with charging components for charging electrically driven vehicles with a corresponding one of the received currents.

Type: Grant
Filed: May 8, 2018
Date of Patent: April 2, 2019
Inventor: Michael Bank

- *System for charging electrically drive vehicles with a single line for transmitting electric current from a source to a charging station*

Patent number: 10250061

Abstract: A system for charging electrically driven vehicles includes a source of three phase electrical current, a first converter converting the three-phase or one-phase electric current received from the source into a converted electric current, a single electric current transmission line transmitting the converted electric current, a second converter converting the converted signal received through the single line into three phase electric current, or one phase electric current, or direct current, and a plurality of charging stations receiving from the second converter corresponding currents and provided with charging components for charging electrically driven vehicles with a corresponding one of the received currents.

Type: Grant
Filed: May 8, 2018
Date of Patent: April 2, 2019
Inventor: Michael Bank

Wide band omni directional antenna

Patent number: 10381744

Abstract: A wide band omni directional antenna, in which the radiation parameters are automatically correspond to the frequency of the emitted signal. It can be made by printing and used in small size transducers, for example in cellular telephones. The antenna radiator is formed as an electrically conductive plate, the electrically

conductive plate which has a shape of a non-rectangular triangle having two lateral sides of different lengths with first ends of the lateral sides connected with one another in a point connectable to an electric signal source and other opposite second ends, and the electrically conductive plate also has a side which is opposite to the point connectable to the electric signal source and connects the opposite second ends of the lateral sides with each other thus forming a third side of the triangle of the non-rectangular triangle. The antenna can be built by using two joined triangles.

Type: Grant
Filed: December 7, 2018
Date of Patent: August 13, 2019
Inventor: Michael Bank

Phase converter for vector conversion of three phase signals

Patent number: 10305289

Abstract: A phase converter for electrical signals is configured for obtaining a vector sum of phase signals or subdividing one signal into several phase signals, including transformers and configured for successive addition of signals received from secondary windings of the transformers and inversion of one or several of the signals, or for subdivision of the one signal into the several phase signals.

Type: Grant
Filed: November 20, 2017
Date of Patent: May 28, 2019
Inventor: Michael Bank

- *SINGLE-WIRE ELECTRIC TRANSMISSION LINE*

Publication number: 20140152123

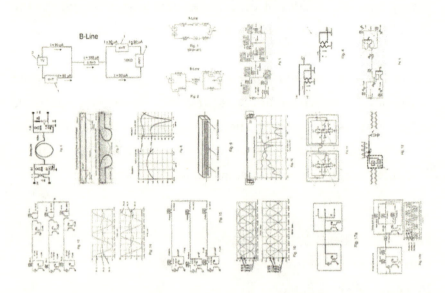

CROSS-REFERENCE TO RELATED APPLICATIONS

This application is a Continuation-in-Part of International Application No. PCT/IL2012/000291 filed Aug. 2, 2012, designating the United States and claiming priority to U.S. Provisional Application No. 61/514,906, filed Aug. 4, 2011, the disclosures of both foregoing applications being incorporated herein by reference in their entireties.

FIELD OF THE INVENTION

The present invention relates to the field of electrical system. More particularly, the invention relates to an electrical transmission system which uses only a single-wire electric transmission line while eliminating the need to use the ground or another wire as commonly used as a second line.

BACKGROUND OF THE INVENTION

Usually in books, articles, or lectures authors explain the work of an electrical circuit (A-Line) as the process of current flowing from the generator to the load by one wire, and then back to the generator by another wire. But it is known that free-access electrons move relatively slowly, and the electrical energy is transmitted at light speed. Actually today's wires electric system uses two or more channels (wires) for transmitting energy or information. While in both channels there is the same information. It is known that active (real) power does not return from load to the generator. From this point of view may be does not need second channel in electrical system. In other words may be a line of electric system can be a single wire.

In the prior-art, there were attempts to perform electrical energy transmission by means of one wire. First applications of the single-wire electrical energy transmission were disclosed by Nikola Tesla in U.S. Pat. No. 1,119,736 and in British Patent No. 8,200. Another single line transmission technique is known as the Goubau line or G-line for short, which is a type of single-wire transmission line which is used at UHF and microwave frequencies (see Geog Goubau, "Surface waves and their Application to Transmission Lines," Journal of Applied Physics, Volume 21, November, 1950). However, a G-line is a type of waveguide, rather than a wire in an electric circuit. There was experiment based on the Russian patent application 1993 year by Stanislav and Konstantin Avramenko [6–8}. All these proposals are based on signal processing like frequency up converting or signal straightening. These processing influences on transmitting information and lead to power lose.

There is also an electricity distribution method using only one conductor, but with the participation of earth. This method is known as the Single Wire Earth Return (SWER). However, the simplification of the energy transfer in this system is achieved due to the loss of half the power produced by the source.

It is well known advantages of three-phase system where energy transmitted by four wires. The presence of four wires is not the only drawback of three-phase system. Another drawback may be the fact that line voltage between two wires in this system at the root of the three above of phase voltage. This may have negative consequences, given such a corona effect and additional losses in the lines.

It is an object of the present invention to provide an electric system which is capable of using a single-wire channel for transmitting energy or information without signal form changing and additional loses.

It is another object of the present invention to provide an electrical system that does not use the ground instead of the second wire.

Other objects and advantages of the invention will become apparent as the description proceeds.

SUMMARY OF THE INVENTION

The present invention relates to a single-wire electric transmission line system, which comprises:

The present invention further relates to a single-wire electric transmission line system, which comprises two phase-shifting devices, coupled to each of the poles of the power source in such a manner that each of said phase-shifting device shifts the phase of a first signal propagating through said pole and the phase of a second signal propagating through the other pole such that the shifted phases of both signals will be essentially identical, and such that the shifted signals are added with essentially the same phase, whenever both poles are connected together to form a single-wire, through which the resulting added signal propagates.

According to an embodiment of the invention, the phase-shifting device(s) is an inverter that shifts the phase of its corresponding pole by +90 degrees, −90 degrees or by 180 degrees, such that the shifted signal(s) is added with essentially the same phase.

According to an embodiment of the invention, the phase-shifting device is a transformer with opposite windings.

According to an embodiment of the invention, one of the two phase-shifting devices is a Low Pass Filter (LPF) and the other phase-shifting device is a High Pass Filter (HPF).

According to an embodiment of the invention, the phase-shifting device is an essentially half period delay line with respect to the length of the line that is connected to the other pole of the source. For example, the delay line is one-port strip line including metal wire on dielectric, which lying on a metallic padding.

According to an embodiment of the invention, the phase-shifting device(s) is a digital module adapted for performing phase shifting. For example, the digital module is a Hilbert transform device.

According to an embodiment of the invention, in the case of a DC signal, the phase-shifting device runs as two capacitors connected in turn to charge through the keys to one of the outputs of a bipolar DC power supply, a second end connected to the power of the capacitor is grounded, the end of the capacitor disconnected from the source, who at the time of charging was grounded is connected to another output bipolar DC power supply and to the input of a single-line, the other end of the capacitor is grounded.

According to an embodiment of the invention, the single-wire is connected to a corresponding single-wire load module that includes a two polar load and phase-shifting device coupled to one polar of said load, by splitting said single-wire into two lines, such that one line is coupled to said phase-shifting device and the other line is coupled to the load, in such a manner that currents are flow in both lines, but in opposite phases with respect to one another.

According to an embodiment of the invention, the single-wire is split into three wires, wherein each of said three wires is connected to a different pole of a three-phase load via a corresponding phase-shifting device, in order to form a single-wire three-phase system, in the following manner:

According to an embodiment of the invention, the first phase-shifting device of the three-phase system is an inductance resistance and the second phase-shifting device of said three-phase system is a capacitor resistance.

In another aspect the invention relates to a single-wire load (instead of ordinary two wires load), which comprises:

BRIEF DESCRIPTION OF THE DRAWINGS

In the drawings:

FIG. 1 schematically illustrates an example of conventional electric system (A-line), according to the prior-art;

FIG. 2 schematically illustrates a single-wire electric system (B-Line) that is equivalent to the A-line system of FIG. 1, according to an embodiment of the present invention;

FIG. 3 is a print out of the simulation results of the B-Line system of FIG. 2;

FIG. 4 schematically illustrates a phase-shifting device in form of a transformer, according to an embodiment of the present invention;

FIG. 5 is a print out of the simulation result of a B-Line system with the transformer of FIG. 4;

FIG. 6 schematically illustrates a scheme of B-Line model with dividing transformers;

FIG. 7 schematically illustrates a conventional high frequency long line and its B-Line equivalent implementation;

FIG. 8 the simulation results of the long line and its B-Line equivalent of FIG. 7;

FIG. 9 schematically illustrates an exemplary one-port strip line for frequency of 2.3 GHz;

FIG. 10 is a graph showing the B-Line with the one-port strip line for frequency 2.3 GHz of FIG. 9 and its simulations results;

FIG. 11 schematically illustrates an exemplary implementation of a DC B-Line circuit, according to an embodiment of the present invention;

FIG. 12 schematically illustrates using one-pole source principle, according to an embodiment of the present invention;

FIG. 13 schematically illustrates an exemplary implementation of a B-Line three-phase scheme, according to an embodiment of the present invention;

FIG. 14 is a graph showing the simulation results of the B-Line three-phase scheme of FIG. 13;

FIG. 15 schematically illustrates an exemplary implementation of B-Line three-phase scheme with one pole generators, according to an embodiment of the present invention;

FIG. 16 is a graph showing the simulation results of the B-Line three-phase scheme of FIG. 5. 15; and

FIGS. 5.17*a* and 5.17*b* schematically illustrate an exemplary implementation of B-Line three-phase scheme with one pole generators and typical three-phase load.

DETAILED DESCRIPTION OF THE INVENTION

Throughout this description the term "B-Line" is used to indicate an electrical circuit as the process of current flowing from the generator to the load by one wire. This term does not imply any particular arrangement or components, and invention is applicable to all suitable configurations of electrical circuits.

First concept—today one can read another explanation as the process of current flowing. Not like from the generator to the load, and then back to the generator. But this explanation is following: "Two potentials derive from two terminal of source with opposite phases to two terminals of load with light speed." So energy flows in one direction.

Second concept—using ground instead of one wire can be for very short distance only; because the earth resistance is much larger than the resistance of copper. According to the resistance of the earth can be from 5 to 5000 ohms per meter. In many electrical systems grounding is used to potential zeroing. An electrical ground system should have an appropriate current-carrying capability to serve as an adequate zero-voltage reference level. In electronic circuit theory, a "ground" is usually idealized as an infinite source or sink for charge, which can absorb an unlimited amount of current without changing its potential. The current flows into the ground and spreads out in an endless ground, as is the case with a protective earth. In the case of protective grounding, if an accident happens, the current anywhere in the other place does not get. The main characteristic of the grounding resistance is spreading current, i.e., a resistance that the earth (ground) has a current spreading at the site of this current. Land spreading is a ground area that surrounds the grounding electrodes, in which the boundary of the current density is so low that potential, which has virtually no land, depends on the current flowing from the electrodes. That is why outside of this boundary current can always be equated to zero. In other words, if one point of scheme connected to ground, it does not mean that the energy or the information is transmitted to another point scheme, which is also connected to ground. Both points have potential equal zero.

Third concept—If one would like to get adequate electrical energy transmitting system processing, one need to do that source and load can "see" the same resistances. And load current mast is the same that is match to Ohm low.

Reference will now be made to several embodiments of the present invention(s), examples of which are illustrated in the accompanying figures. Wherever practicable similar or like reference numbers may be used in the figures and may indicate similar or like functionality. The figures depict embodiments of the present invention for purposes of illustration only. One skilled in the art will readily recognize from the following description that alternative embodiments of the structures and methods illustrated herein may be employed without departing from the principles of the invention described herein.

The terms, "for example," "e.g.," "optionally," as used herein, are intended to be used to introduce non-limiting examples. While certain references are made to certain example system components or services, other components and services can be used as well and/or the example components can be combined into fewer components and/or divided into further components.

It will be better to explain the main idea of a single-wire electric system of the present invention (i.e., B-Line) by comparison with a conventional electric system (i.e., A-Line). FIGS. 1 and 2 schematically illustrate an A-Line circuit and a B-Line circuit, respectively. Both circuits include a common power source **2** (e.g., 1 volt generator), a load

3 (e.g., R=10 kOhm) and the currents is about 90 microamperes (I≈90 μA). At the A-Line circuit the lines resistance is about 1 kOhm, and at the B-Line circuit, the resistance of the single-wire transmission line is about 0.5 kOhm as will be described in further details hereinafter. The equivalent B-Line circuit includes a first phase shifter **1** coupled to one poles of the power source **2** and a second phase shifter coupled to one of the poles of the load **3**.

The B-Line system of the present invention is based on the assumption that it would be possible to combine two wires (i.e., the electric lines running out from the first pole and the second pole of a power source) if currents would be of the same amplitudes and same phases. For example, this can be achieved by inserting a phase-shifting device (i.e., the phase shifter **1**) in one of the lines. The phase-shifting device shifts the phase of a first signal propagating through that line such that the shifted phase of the first signal will be essentially identical to the phase of a second signal propagating through the other line. For instance, 10 milliseconds delay line can be used for signal with a frequency of 50 Hz. After the phase-shifting device, phases and amplitudes of the currents in both lines are essentially identical. Thus, at the generator side (i.e., at the power source **2** side), both lines can be combined into a single wire, such that the shifted first signal is added to the second signal with essentially the same phase of the second signal, whenever both lines are connected together to form a single-wire, through which the resulting added signal propagates (i.e., the sum of the currents from both lines).

At the load side, the single wire splits into two wires (i.e., two lines), and similarly to the generator side, a phase-shifting device (i.e., a second phase shifter **1**) can be inserted before the load **3** in one of the split wires in order to ensure a normal functionality of the load

3. As a result, the two conventional wire system (FIG. 1) turns into one-way B-Line system (FIG. 2), but the power source **2** and the load **3** will "see" the conventional two wires system (i.e., A-Line).

According to an embodiment of the invention, the needed phase shift can be achieved by means of a phase-shifting device in form of a delay line, a transformer with opposite windings, low pass and high pass filters, digital phase shifters such as Hilbert transform device(s), etc. For example, if a delay line is used as a phase-shifting device, then its delay must correspond to half period. In the case of 50 or 60 Hz frequencies it is practically impossible using delay line, recall that wire, which corresponds to half wave length, has length equals 3000 or 2500 km. It is convenient on low frequencies to use transformer with opposite windings as phase shifter. As for high frequencies the good solution is delay line.

The main idea of the single-wire electric transmission line of the present invention was supported on ADS and CST simulations programs. Series of simulations with different phase shifters and various resistance lines were carried out. Each simulation was carried out for the A-Line and the B-Line. For clarity, FIGS. 1–3 show the conditions and the simulation results including polarity and magnitude of currents.

That's one of the simulations for the verification of Ohm's law in the proposed scheme (see FIG 5.1). In this typical A-Line circuit, current amplitude everywhere should be 90 µA, wherein 0.5 kOhm is the lines resistance.

In the proposed B-Line scheme (see FIG. 2), we added phase two shifting devices the first at the input and the second at the output, and combined the two lines. As a result a line resistance is 0.5 kOhm. The simulation shows that the currents at the input and output have not changed. The polarity of the load current depends on where the phase-shifting devices are at the top or bottom.

One can see on FIG. 3 the simulation results of the B-Line system of FIG. 2. For example, in case the phase-shifting device is a transformer with opposite windings, then reverse one wire current phase by the transformer can be reset the current flowing from the winding only. Simply connect the windings cannot be, otherwise the current from one winding to another will flow and the transformer will not perform its functions. As in other similar cases, zeroing can be done with earth (see "Circuit Grounds and Grounding Practices," George Hunka, Undergraduate Laboratory, Dept. of EE, University of Pennsylvania). As will be shown in the following section, the land is not involved in the transfer of energy from the source to the load.

FIG. 4 schematically illustrates a phase-shifting device that can be used in conjunction with the invention. In this embodiment, the phase-shifting device is in form of a transformer. The phase-shifting device illustrated in this figure is particularly convenient because it can be easily applied to low frequency systems. The phase-shifting device is generally indicated by numeral 1 in the figures.

FIG. 5 is print out that shows the results of a B-Line circuit simulation with two units of inverter **1** (as indicated by the transformers TF**1** and TF**2**). The first transformer TF**2** is coupled to an AC voltage source SRC **1** (as indicated by numeral 2) and the second transformer TF**1** is coupled to the load **3** (as indicated by the resistor RI). One can see on FIG. 5 B-Line circuit with ideal 1:1 transformers simulation.

If the B-Line is used in a system with raising or lowering the voltage, the inverter **1** must be used in both lines. In the one line is used as the transformer with the same included windings (as indicated by transformer TF**2**) and in the second line with opposite included windings (as indicated by transformer TF**1**). The grounding in FIG. 5.5 is zeroing and therefore it is not used and cannot be used as the return path (i.e., the second line). There are several evidences that the earth is not involved in the transfer of power, although one of any evidence would be enough. The main evidence is that the current in B-Line equals to double current in normal scheme and corresponds to Ohm low. So it is impossible any additional current.

Obviously, in the case of a normal two-wire circuit where the source gives 1 V and a load resistance is 50 ohms the current will be equal to 20 mA. For example, in the case of the B-Line circuit like in FIG. 5.5 the current in wire should be 40 mA.

With the aim of experimental verification of the proposed solutions were prepared a number of models. Details of the layout mounted on a wooden board, as a zeroing-grounding used electrical network protective grounding. All voltages and currents in the model coincided with the results of the simulation. To eliminate possible doubts about the possible involvement of the land in signal transduction through the neutral wire three-phase system was tested model with dividing (isolating) transformer at the input. This model scheme is shown in FIG. 6. The model shown in FIG. 6 continued to operate normally and when it was taken out of the receiving part of the laboratory at a distance of about 80 meter and used as a grounding metal rod.

B-Line on High Frequency

Let us show that B-line idea is correct for the high frequency too. On frequency 50 Hz simulations where made by ADS program. This program allows simulating different elements but not electrical lines. So for electrical lines simulations was used element like delay line. On height frequencies one can implement CST program. This program allows simulating different elements including electrical lines.

First we compare normal long line with characteristic impedance 300 Ohm with B-Line on frequency 1.1 GHz. Both models are shown in FIG. 5.7, wherein FIG. 8 shows the simulation results of models 1 and 2 of FIG. 7, on frequency of 1 GHz (as indicated by parameters S11 and S21). On 1.1 GHz it was possible to make delay lines by lines with long equals half wave long. Parameter S21 is the same practically. Parameter S11 of model 2 is better than S11 of model 1. One can see on FIG. 8 on 1.1 GHz S11 of B-Line is −20 dB and of normal long line is −10 dB. This means that in case of B-line all energy goes from source to load (i.e., there is no power loss).

In high frequency it is possible to make delay line like one-port strip line, e.g., as shown with respect to FIG. 9. With this strip line was made simulation of one wire long line. The simulation results in terms of S-parameter (S1 and S2) magnitude (in dB) are shown in the graph of FIG. 10. The matching long the line is infinitely wide band passes (see appendix about eternal resonance system). This is an advantage, but also disadvantages. There is an advantage because you can pass on a long line of multiple signals with different frequencies. However, in a real system there is always some noise. Even if noise is weak, but in an infinitely wide band it will be infinitely large noise (of course, if the noise is white). Of course, you can apply a filter at the input of the receiver. But this is often problematic. The filter introduces loss and increases the noise factor.

The proposed single-wire system (B-Line) is a selective system. The disadvantage of B-Line is a need to change the delay line in case of change of frequency. B-Line is compatible with the source and load, and in this sense no different from the usual long line. It is selective, but rather broadband. It has no requirements of symmetry, which is often a problem in the prior-art systems when using long line inside the apparatus, where can be different influences on each wire. and DC B-Line

To implement the inverter **1** in a DC circuitry it requires a different solution then the aforementioned transformers. According to an embodiment of the invention, it is proposed to use two capacitors and corresponding switches to implement the inverter **1** (as shown with respect to FIG. 11 in the source side **2** and correspondingly at the load side **3**). Each of the inverter **1** operates as follows: In one period the first capacitor is charges and the second is discharged. In second period they switch functions. Charging current is in one direction, but discharging current direction is reversed.

In this embodiment, in line current has one direction, positive or negative. In this figure, the direction is positive. The resistance value is usually set. So first and second period's duration can only be choosing by value of the capacitors. For example, such a DC B-Line system can be implemented in an electrical railway system (i.e., tramway). In this case, it is possible to transmit electrical power only in wire or only in the rails.

One-Pole Source

The idea of B-Line system allows defining another new element of an electrical circuit—one-pole generator (i.e., source). If we will allocate the connection of the generator and the converter in B-Line scheme, we can talk about unipolar source (as indicated by dotted line in FIG. 5. 12) where one load terminal is connected to a single-wire and the second load terminal is grounded (connected to zero voltage). In this case there is no loss of energy, as all the current coming from a single line passes through the load.

B-Line (One wire) Three-Phase Systems

According to some embodiment of the invention, the suggested B-Line concept allows building unbalanced three-phase system where currents in all phases do not depend on loads in another phases. FIG. 5.13 schematically illustrates a B-Line three-phase scheme with loads 10, 50 and 200 Ohm. Moreover, this B-Line three-phase scheme uses three wires only. The simulation results of this B-Line three-phase scheme are shown in FIG. 5.15). The simulation results on FIG. 14 show that each current depends only on its load, but not like in common three-phase system.

According to another embodiment of the invention, the B-Line three-phase system can be built without using of inverters in the receiving parts (as shown with respect to FIG. 15 and to its corresponding simulation results as shown in FIG. 16). Actually this scheme uses one pole generators. As one can see in the graph of FIG. 16, the current values are by two times smaller than currents value in scheme with reflectors in receiving parts. But generators currents are smaller by two times too. Therefore there is no power loses in this scheme too. It is possible to combine one-pole source through one wire with normal three-phase load by implementing 1200 phase shifters, as seen in FIGS. 5. 17a– 5.17 b.

According to another embodiment, the single-wire may be split into three wires, where each of the three wires is connected to a different pole of a three-phase load via a corresponding phase-shifting device, in order to form a single-wire three-phase system. Accordingly, a first phase-shifting device is coupled to one of the poles of the three-phase load in such a manner that the first phase-shifting device shifts the phase of a first signal propagating through the pole by +60° (e.g., by using a filter). A second phase-shifting device is coupled to the second pole of the three-phase toad in such a manner that the second phase-shifting device shifts the phase of a second signal propagating through the second pole by –60° (e.g., by using a filter). A third phase-shifting device is coupled to the third pole of the three-phase load in such a manner that the third phase-shifting device shifts the phase of a third signal propagating through the third pole by 180° (e.g., by using an inverter). This way, a phase shift of 120° between signals is obtained with minimal energy loss (compared to shifting the phase of the signals by 120° using filters), since the filters are used to shift the phase of the signals only by ±60°.

It should be indicated that if it is desired to protect power lines (cables) there is an option to use a technique where conventional 3 phase high-voltage power lines which extend along a pipe and buried in the ground. However, the high voltage between phases requires substantially separating between them and therefore, the only solution is using 3 insulating pipes (each cable in a separate pipe), to allow sufficient distance between pipes, such that the electric and magnetic field of each line will not induce disturbing currents in the neighboring lines. However, this solution is costly, due to the fact that it is impossible to put all 3 cables in a single pipe. The single-wire electric transmission line system, proposed by the present invention allows using a single high voltage cable (carrying 3 phases) which is extended along a single insulating pipe and buried in the ground, since there are no neighboring lines. This way, the power line is protected against falling trees, rain and falling snow, with relatively low cost, comparing to the need to bury 3 lines.

As will be appreciated by the skilled person the arrangement described in the figures results in an electrical circuit which uses only a single-wire electric transmission line. One-Way system for connection between source and load by one line—(i.e., B-Line) was proposed and checked by simulations and experiments. One way system can be easily implemented as One-pole source, DC B-Line, LF B-Line, HF B-Line, B-Line three-phase system, etc.

It is possible to suppose that using one-way method (i.e., B-Line) can considerable decrease the electrical lines cost. Moreover, B-Line method allows decreasing energy loss in high-voltage electric transmission lines. An additional advantage provided by the invention is that it is possible to achieve decreasing of electrical lines radiation, including Corona effect, so far as one of radiation courses in two lines and three-phase systems have high voltage between lines. Furthermore, B-Line method allows simplifying the high-frequency long lines and improving their options, including easing the requirements for symmetry, good matching and selective properties. Finally, B-Line method also allows building antennas with one radiated element (monopole) equivalent to two element antenna (dipole).

All the above description and examples have been given for the purpose of illustration and are not intended to limit the invention in any way. Many different mechanisms, methods of analysis, electronic and logical elements can be employed, all without exceeding the scope of the invention.

Claims (7)

1. A single-wire electric transmission line system that is composed of the following:

    a. a power source having first and second poles

    b. a phase-shifting device, coupled to one of the poles of said power source so that said phase-shifting device shifts the phase of a first signal propagating through said pole and the shifted phase of said first signal will be essentially identical to the phase of a second signal propagating through the other pole, and such that the shifted first signal is added to the second signal with essentially the same phase of second signal, whenever both poles are connected together to form a single wire through which the resulting added signal propagates

    c. two phase-shifting devices, coupled to each of the poles of said power source in such a manner that each of said phase-shifting device shifts the phase of a first signal propagating through said pole and the phase of a second signal propagating through the other pole such that the shifted phases of both signals will be essentially identical, and such that the shifted signals are added with essentially the same phase, when both poles are connected together to form a single wire through which the resulting added signal propagates

d. a two-polar load, wherein the single wire is split before the load into two lines, with one of the lines connected to one pole of the load directly to transmit a current to the one pole of the load, while the other of the lines is connected to the load via a phase-shifting device that shifts a phase of another current relative to a phase of the one current and transmits another current with the shifted phase to the load.

2. A single-wire electric transmission line system according to claim 1, in which the phase-shifting device is an inverter that shifts the phase of its corresponding pole by +90 degrees, by −90 degrees, or by 180 degrees, such that the shifted signal is added with essentially the same phase.

3. A system according to claim 1, in which the phase-shifting device is a transformer with opposite windings.

4. A system according to claim 1, in which the phase-shifting device is a half-period delay line with respect to the length of the line that is connected to the other pole of the source.

5. A system according to claim 4, in which the delay line is a one-port strip line including metal wire on dielectric, which delay line lying on the metallic padding.

6. A system according to claim 1, in which the phase-shifting device is a digital module adapted for performing a phase shifting.

7. A system according to claim 6, in which the digital module is a Hilbert transform device.

From other one wire patents

Wideband omni-directional antenna

Patent number: 10381744

Abstract: A wideband Omni-directional antenna, in which the radiation parameters automatically correspond to the frequency of the emitted signal. It can be made by printing and used in small-size transducers, for example, in cellular telephones. The antenna radiator is formed as an electrically conductive plate, which has a shape of a nonrectangular triangle having two lateral sides of different lengths with first ends of the lateral sides connected with one another in a point connectable to an electric signal source and other opposite second ends, and the electrically conductive plate also has a side that is opposite to the point connectable to the electric signal source and connects the opposite second ends of the lateral sides with each other, thus forming a third side of the triangle of the nonrectangular triangle. The antenna can be built by using two joined triangles.

–   US *Patent* No. US6297971B1

05289. Phase converter for vector conversion of three-phase signals

A phase converter for electrical signals is configured for obtaining a vector sum of phase signals or subdividing one signal into several phase signals, including transformers, and configured for successive addition of signals received from secondary windings of the transformers and inversion of one or several of the signals, or for subdivision of one signal into several phase signals.

Step-up and step-down transformers and results of the simulation according to the present invention.

Description of the Preferred Embodiments

The converter according to the present invention is designed to operate on the basis of a vector synthesis.

It is known that in a three-phase electrical energy transmission system, the electrical energy is transmitted through three lines or wires, and phases of electrical signals are offset from each other by 120°. To obtain a single-phase signal, the three-phase signal is separated into three signals, and they are used for different loads.

It is, however, sometimes necessary to convert the whole three-phase signal into one single-phase signal (two-wire signal). For example, it takes place when it is required to supply the whole power supplied from the three-phase system to one single-phase load. This is not possible to achieve by simple summation of the three signals because a sum of the three signals that are offset from each other by 120° is equal to zero.

The converter according to the present invention is configured so that it makes possible a conversion of a three-phase signal into a single-phase (two-wire) signal, or into a single-wire signal, and vice versa.

The convertor according to the present invention for converting a three-phase signal into a single wire signal is symbolically shown in Figure 1.

The convertor according to the present invention for converting a single-wire signal into a three-phase is symbolically shown in Figure 2.

The convertor according to the present invention for converting a three-phase signal into a single-phase signal is symbolically shown in Figure 3.

The convertor according to the present invention for converting a single-phase signal into a three-phase signal is symbolically shown in Figure 4.

The convertor according to the present invention for converting a three-phase signal into a single wire signal is symbolically shown in Figure 1, which is designed, for example, as follows. It is known that the phases of signals or currents in a three-phase system are offset from each other by 120°, as shown in Figure 5.

For obtaining from the three-phase signal of one single-line or single-wire signal, the direction of a vector of one of the currents is changed to an opposite direction, for example, that of vector **3**. As a result, the angles of all vectors are obtained, as shown in Figure 6. Then all three vectors are summated.

It is shown below that when the converter according to the present invention uses the above-described method, which is carried out by, it will not lead to any losses.

For a three-phase system, the following is known:

1. A sum of three signals in a three-phase system is equal to zero.

2. It is known that the power of a balanced three-phase system is equal to the sum of the powers of three phases.

Let us summate two vectors of voltages (1 and 2) with phases offset by 120°:

$V\Sigma^2=V1^2+V2^2+2V1^*V2\ Cos\ (\Delta\varphi)$
Cos 120°=−0.5 Cos 60°=0.5
For V1=V2=V and Δφ=120°
$V\Sigma^2=V^2+V^2-V^*V=V^2$

It can be seen that the value of the summated vector is equal to the value of each of the vectors V. There were two signals with phases + and −60° and voltages of the source V. They were united, and this means that a signal is obtained with a phase equal to 0 and voltage V.

Figure 7 shows the currents that are produced by two vectors 1 and 2 separately, while Figure 8 shows the summated power after uniting the two vectors. In other words, the summated voltage after uniting the two vectors 1 and 2 is equal to 2 V. The value of the sum of the two vectors of voltages is equal to V. This means that the sums of three vectors in Figure 5 will be equal to 0. The power of the three phases will be equal to 3VI, since the current in the common wire will be equal to the triple-phase current. This means that both conditions of a three-phase system are satisfied.

Figure 9 shows a converter C1-3 according to the present invention, which realizes the summation of all three vectors. The three-phase source **9.1** gives the energy to two transformers **9.2** and **9.3**. A transformer **9.3** is introduced, with the use of an opposite connection of the windings, which actually corresponds to the nullifiers of the inventor. The secondary windings of all three transformers are connected in series for the addition of all three vectors.

As can be seen from Figure 9, there are no phase shifters of the types LR or CR. There are only transformers that do not change the power of the signals.

This means that the operation of the converter **3-1** does not depend on changes of load values.

The converter C**3-2** in Figure 10 can be made by connecting to the converter **3-1** of an additional transformer.

The converter C**1-3**, which uses a capacitor, uses the concept of vector synthesis according to the present invention for the conversion of a single-line or single-wire signal into a three-phase signal in a manner particularly illustrated in Figure 11 of the drawing.

Vector V is supplied to the input of the converter C**1-3**, and it converts vector V into vectors A, B, C having phase shifts between them of 120°. Vector A (**11.3**) is obtained by turning a phase of a copy of vector V by 60° by means of a capacitor, whose reactive resistance is greater than the active resistance of a load of the converter. Vector B (**11.2**) is obtained as a result of the inversion of vector V. Vector C (**11.1**) is obtained by a vector addition of copies of vectors A and B (**11.3**).

Figure 12 shows an electrical scheme of the converter C**1-3** with the use of a capacitor **12.1**. It includes transformers **12.2, 12.3, 12.4,** and **12.5**. The transformer **12.3** is introduced into the system with the opposite windings **12.4, 12.5,** and **12.6** of the loads of the three-phase system A, B, and C. The current in the transformer **12.5** is a vector sum of currents of the load C and B after the inversion and the input current after inversion. The current in the load B is an inverted current of the input signal. Element **12.1** is a capacitor whose reactive resistance is greater than the active resistance of the load C.

The converter **C1-3**, which uses inductance, uses the concept of vector synthesis according to the present invention for the conversion of a single-line or single-wire signal into a three-shape signal in a manner particularly illustrated in Figure 13 of the drawing. Vector V is supplied to the input of the converter **C1-3**, and it converts vector V into vectors A, B, and C having phase shifts between them of 120°. Vector A (**13.1**) is obtained by turning a phase of a copy of vector V by 60° by means of an inductance, whose reactive resistance is greater than the active resistance of a load of the converter. Vector B (**13.2**) is obtained as a result of the inversion of the vector V. Vector C (**13.3**) is obtained by a vector addition of copies of vectors A and B.

Figure 14 shows an electrical scheme of the converter **C1-3** with the use of an inductor **14.5**. It includes transformers **14.1, 14.2, 13.3**, and **14.4**. The transformer **14.1** is introduced into the system with the opposite windings. The current in the transformer **12.4** is a vector sum of currents of the loads A and B after the inversion. The current in the load B is an inverted current of the input signal. Element **14.51** is an inductor whose reactive resistance is greater than the active resistance of the load.

The converter **C3-1** can be realized as is shown by stimulation according to the program ADC in Figure 15. It includes the same elements as in Figure 10 but in a form required for stimulation.

The simulation results in Figure 15 show that the sum of the powers of the three phases at the converter input is equal to the signal power on the load. That is, in the case of ideal transformers, this converter operates without loss.

Figure 16 shows a scheme and results of the simulation of the connection of two converters C3-1 and C1-3. Increasing and reducing transformers are introduced between them in the single-wire line.

The values of currents and input data show that the powers supplied from the three-phase source are equal to the powers on the loads.

As a zeroing unit or a ground, it is recommended to use a nullifier. If the resistance of the nullifier is close to zero, then the currents entering it will not cause energy losses. The resistance of the nullifier can be of any low value if several nullifiers connected in parallel are utilized. In this case, a current from the nullifier does not propagate into the ground.

The construction and the operation of the nullifier are disclosed in M. Bank *It Is Quite Another Electricity*, second edition, revised, Partridge Publishing, 2017. The present invention is not limited to the details shown since various modifications and structural changes are possible without departing from the spirit of the invention. What is desired to be protected by Letters Patent is set forth in the appended claims.

Claims

1. A phase converter for electrical signals, comprising means for obtaining a vector sum of phase signals or subdividing one signal into several phase signals, said means including transformers configured for successive addition of signals received from secondary windings of the transformers and inversion of one or

several of the signals, or for subdivision of one signal into several phase signals, where in one or in several of the transformers a secondary winding is switched opposite to its prime winding forming an inverted signal, and in said one or several transformers in which the secondary winding is switched opposite to the prime winding forming the inverted signal the secondary winding and the primary winding have a common point connected to a nullifier or a grounding, while the secondary windings of some of the transformers are connected in series.

2. A phase converter for the electrical signals of claim 1, wherein said means include an additional transformer with a primary winding connected between an outlet of the converter and the nullifier or the grounding and a secondary winding with both ends representing the outlet of the converter.

3. A phase converter for electrical signals, comprising means for obtaining a vector sum of phase signals or subdividing one signal into several phase signals, said means including transformers configured for successive addition of signals received from secondary windings of the transformers and inversion of one or several of the signals, or for subdivision of one signal into several phase signals, where in one or in several of the transformers a secondary winding is switched opposite to its first winding forming an inverted signal, while the secondary windings of some of the transformers are connected in series, further comprising an input, wherein a single signal, which is vector V, is supplied to the input of the converter. The single signal is divided into three signals including first, second, and third. The first vector is obtained by turning a phase of the sector V by 60° by a capacitor or an inductance winding whose reactive resistance is greater

than a reactive resistance of a load of the converter. The second vector is obtained by inverting a copy of the vector V. The third vector is obtained by a vector addition of copies of the first and second vectors.

Charging a One-Wire System

US patent 10,250,661.System for charging electrically driven vehicles with a single line.

- <u>Electrical energy transmission system which does not require reservation</u>

Patent number: 11258268

- <u>Phase converter for vector conversion of three-phase signals</u>

Patent number: 10305289

Abstract: A phase converter for electrical signals is configured for obtaining a vector sum of phase signals or subdividing one signal into several phase signals, including transformers, and configured for successive addition of signals received from the secondary windings of the transformers and inversion of one or several of the signals, or for subdivision of one signal into several phase signals.

- <u>Phase converter for vector conversion of three-phase signals</u>

Publication number: 20190157875

Abstract: A phase converter for electrical signals is configured for obtaining a vector sum of phase signals or subdividing one signal into several phase signals, including transformers and configured for successive addition of signals received from secondary windings of the transformers and inversion of one or several of the signals, or for subdivision of the one signal into the several phase signals.

- <u>System for charging electrically driven vehicles with a single line for transmitting electric current from a source to a charging station</u>

Patent number: 10250061

Abstract: A system for charging electrically driven vehicles includes a source of three-phase electrical current, a first converter converting the three-phase or one-phase electric current received from the source into a converted electric current, a single electric current transmission line transmitting the converted electric current, a second converter converting the converted signal received through the single line into three-phase electric current or one-phase electric current or direct current, and a plurality of charging stations receiving from the second converter corresponding currents and provided with charging components for charging electrically driven vehicles with a corresponding one of the received currents.

<u>Wideband antenna</u>

- US Patent 9246405B2

Electrical Energy Transmission System with a Single Transmission Line

Abstract

An electrical energy transmission system has a three-phase electric current power source that generates a three-phase electric current having three electric currents, a converting device that converts the three-phase electric current to obtain a common electric current signal formed by the summation of three electric currents having the same phases, and a single-line electrical transmission line that transmits further the thusly produced common electric current signal.

Images (11)

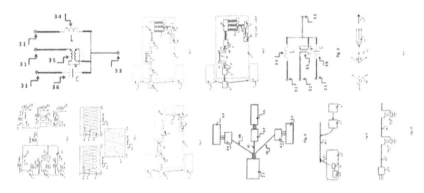

Figures E

United States
Inventor: <u>Michael Bank</u>

Cross-Reference to Related Applications

- <u>2.4 Phase Converter</u>

Abstract

A phase converter that converts single-phase AC electric power to balanced three-phase AC power. Two input terminals connected to the output of a single-phase AC power source connect directly to two output terminals of the converter. The phase converter has two serially connected storage capacitors with a common connection, a charging circuit for controlled charging the storage capacitors and an output circuit for controlled discharge of the storage capacitors to provide single -phase AC power to a third output terminal. The charging circuit controls input to the storage capacitor to provide a sinusoidal input current and to step up the voltage to the storage capacitors. The output circuit provides output power to the third output terminal of a predetermined phase and amplitude, relative to the other two output terminals, to result in balanced three-phase AC power at the three output terminals. The phase converter provides a balanced three-phase output for leading power factor, lagging power factor, and resistive loads.

Images (6)

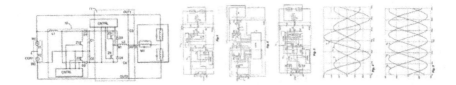

- **Phase converter for vector conversion of three phase signals**

Patent number: 10305289

Abstract: A phase converter for electrical signals is configured for obtaining a vector sum of phase signals or subdividing one signal into several phase signals, including transformers and configured for successive addition of signals received from secondary windings of the transformers and inversion of one or several of the signals, or for subdivision of the one signal into the several phase signals.

Type: Grant
Filed: November 20, 2017
Date of Patent: May 28, 2019
Inventor: Michael Bank

- *System for charging electrically drive vehicles with a single line for transmitting electric current from a source to a charging station*

number: 10250061

Abstract: A system for charging electrically driven vehicles includes a source of three phase electrical current, a first converter converting the three-phase or one-phase electric current received from the source into a converted electric current, a single electric current transmission line transmitting the converted electric current, a second converter converting the converted signal received through the single line into three phase electric current, or one phase electric current, or direct current, and a plurality of charging stations receiving from the second converter corresponding currents and provided with charging components for charging electrically driven vehicles with a corresponding one of the received currents.

Type: Grant
Filed: May 8, 2018
Date of Patent: April 2, 2019

Inventor: Michael Bank

Filed: November 20, 2017

Date of Patent: May 28, 2019

Inventor: Michael Bank

- *PHASE CONVERTER FOR VECTOR CONVERSION OF THREE PHASE SIGNALS*

Publication number: 20190157875

Abstract: A phase converter for electrical signals is configured for obtaining a vector sum of phase signals or subdividing one signal into several phase signals, including transformers and configured for successive addition of signals received from secondary windings of the transformers and inversion of one or several of the signals, or for subdivision of the one signal into the several phase signals.

Type: Application

Filed: November 20, 2017

Publication date: May 23, 2019

Inventor: Michael Bank

Patent number: 10381744

Inventor: Michael Bank

- *Phase converter for vector conversion of three phase signals*

Patent number: 10305289

Abstract: A phase converter for electrical signals is configured for obtaining a vector sum of phase signals or subdividing one signal into several phase signals, including transformers and configured for successive addition of signals received from secondary windings of

the transformers and inversion of one or several of the signals, or for subdivision of the one signal into the several phase signals.

Type: Grant
Filed: November 20, 2017

Abstract: A surface antenna with a single radiation element, which comprises (a) a power source with first and second poles; (b) a phase shifting element, inserted to the path of one of the poles of the power source in such a manner that the phase shifting device shifts the phase of a first signal propagating through said pole such that the shifted phase of the first signal will be essentially identical to the phase of a second signal propagating through the other pole. The shifted first signal is added to the second signal with essentially the same phase of second signal, whenever both poles are connected together to form a single-wire, through which the resulting added signal propagates.

Patent number: 9246405

Abstract: An electrical energy transmission system has a three-phase electric current power source which generates a three-phase electric current having three electric currents, a converting device which converts the three-phase electric current to obtain a common electric current signal formed by summation of three electric currents having the same phases, and a single-line electrical transmission line which transmits further the thusly produced common electric current signal.

ATIONAL, LLC
Inventor: Michael Bank

ELECTRICAL ENERGY TRANSMISSION SYSTEM

Publication number: 20150229232

Abstract: An electrical energy transmission system has a three-phase electric current power source which generates a three-phase electric current having three electric currents, a converting device which converts the three-phase electric current to obtain a common electric current signal formed by summation of three electric currents having the same phases, and a single-line electrical transmission line which transmits further the thusly produced common electric current signal.

Inventor: Michael Bank

Abstract: An electric energy transmission system which does not need a reservation has a generator generating a multi-phase electric current, a converter converting it into another electric current, an electric current network connected with the converter and having a first group of electric current lines extending towards electric current users and a second group of electric current ones electrically connecting the electric current lines of the first group with each other, and a plurality of consumer blocks connected with the network and having users which use different electric currents and further converters converting the electric current transmitted by the network into the different electric currents and supplying the different electric currents to the electric current users.

Type: Grant

13, 2019

- *Phase converter for vector conversion of three phase signals*

Patent number: 10305289

Abstract: A phase converter for electrical signals is configured for obtaining a vector sum of phase signals or subdividing one signal into several phase signals, including transformers and configured for successive addition of signals received from secondary windings of the transformers and inversion of one or several of the signals, or for subdivision of the one signal into the several phase signals.

Type: Grant
Filed: November 20, 2017
Date of Patent: May 28, 2019
Inventor: Michael Bank

Instead of concluded – one of possible implementations.

Possibly one of the causes of world heating in the last hundred years is electrical wires. Today around the globe there are many three phase lines, transmitting large energy quantities. One of the advantages of a three-phase system is the absence of a radiating electromagnetic field, if the line is balanced.

But wires in these systems work under high temperatures of about 100 degrees. The heating radiating is summing with the heating of the sun. The impact of this heating will be more strong on poleses due to temperature differences.

For decreasing this addition heating one can use one wire method instead of three phase method. As shown in [19], this method allows transmitting the same quantity of energy as in a three-phase line. Using three wires can transmit by three times energy more than in today using three phase systems.

References

1. Shannon, C.E. "The Mathematical Theory of Communication." *Bell Syst. Tech. J.*27 (1948), Pages: 379–423, 623–656.

2. Blahut, R.E. *Principles and Practice of Information Theory.* Addison-Wealey, 1987.

3. Hamming, R.W. *Coding and Information Theory.* Prentice-Hall, 1980.

4. Lubbe, Jan C. A. van der *Information Theory.* Cambridge University Press, 2002.

5. ownsend, B. *PAL Color Television.* Cambridge University Press, 1970.

6. Watkinson, J. *The Art of Digital Video.*Focal Press, 2000.

7. Zwicker, E.,and H. Fastl. *Psychoacoustics: Facts and Models.* Springer-Verlag, 1990.

8. Bank, M. "Bearbeitung der schallinformationimmenschlichengehorsystem und in

technischen anlagen." *RundfunktechnischenMittelungen*, N2 (1992): 53–65.

9. Bank, M., and U. Mahlab. "Hearing System Model and Sound Quality Estimation." *WSEAS Transactions on Acoustics and Music* 1, no. 1 (2004): 34–44.

10. Bank, M. "Video and Audio Compressions and Human Perception Mechanism." Plenary lecture on 2nd WSEAS International Conference on Communications.

11. Human perception seminar in www.OFDMA-MANFRED. comWSEAS *Transactions on Communications*Michael Bank ISSN: 1109-2742 764 Issue 7, Volume 7, July 2008.

12. Bank, M. *It Is Quite Another Electricity, Transmitting by One Wire and Without Grounding, second edition* (Partridge, 2023).

www.ingramcontent.com/pod-product-compliance
Lightning Source LLC
Chambersburg PA
CBHW051231050326
40689CB00007B/883